What Are Your Travel Plans?

Human beings are careless. They misplace things They get lost. And sometimes, they can't find their way back ... to the *future*. Trapped in layers of rock, sediment, silt, tar, and clay, they lie entombed for millions and millions of years, waiting for archaeologists to discover them.

Prehistoric anachronisms, skeletal remains, and artifacts from long before humanity existed on the planet continue to amass around the world as scientists unearth evidence in support of time travel. J. H. Brennan presents the finds, arguments, and theories for the existence of time travel in *Time Travel: A New Perspective*.

As each chapter unfolds, your world view will change forever. This riveting book is based on sound scientific evidence, yet the conclusions themselves have the excitement of the wildest science fiction. Get ready for an unforgettable trip in time. What are you waitng for? The future has arrived ... millions of years ago.

About the Author

J. H. Brennan is an acclaimed author of fifty-two books of fiction and non-fiction, several of which have become international bestsellers. His works have appeared in more than fifty countries of Europe, Asia, North and South America, and Australia. His GrailQuest™ series of adventure gamebooks for young readers is a phenomenal success worldwide.

Brennan started his intellectual journey at an early age, studying psychology virtually from the time he could read, and hypnotizing a school friend at age nine! At twenty-four, he was the youngest newspaper editor in his native Ireland. By his mid-twenties, he had published his first novel, and his out-of-body experience work *Astral Doorways* is a classic in its field.

Herbie Brennan is clearly an active man of ideas. In addition to his work as an author, he maintains a career as a consultant in financial marketing, as well as an active interest in software development, self-improvement techniques, and reincarnational research. He is a frequent lecturer and media guest throughout the United Kingdom and Ireland.

Also by J.H. Brennan

Astral Doorways (Aquarian Press)
Experimental Magic (Aquarian Press)
Reincarnation (Aquarian Press)
Occult Reich (Futura)
The Ultimate Elsewhere (Futura)
An Occult History of the World (Futura)
Nostradamus—Visions of the Future (Harper/Collins)
Ancient Spirit (Little, Brown)
Mindreach (Aquarian Press)
Discover Reincarnation (Harper/Collins)
Discover Astral Projection (Harper/Collins)
A Guide to Megalithic Ireland (Harper/Collins)
With Eileen Campbell:
Aquarian Guide to the New Age (Harper/Collins)

Time Travel

A New Perspective

J. H. Brennan

1997
Llewellyn Publications
St. Paul, Minnesota, U.S.A. 55164-0383

FIRST EDITION
First Printing, 1997

Cover design: Tom Grewe
Photo research: Jo Wagner
Editing: Laura Gudbaur
Book design and project management: Ken Schubert

Library of Congress Cataloging-in-Publication Data

Brennan, J. H.
　　Time Travel : a new perspective / J. H. Brennan. -- 1st ed.
　　　　p.　　cm.
　　Includes bibliographical references and index.
　　ISBN 1-56718-235-6 (trade pbk.)
　　1. Time reversal.　2. Paleontology.　I. Title.
　　QC173.59.T53B74　　1997
　　133.8--dc21　　　　　　　　　　　　　　　　96- 51653
　　　　　　　　　　　　　　　　　　　　　　　　　　CIP

Printed in the United States of America

Llewellyn Publications
A Division of Llewellyn Worldwide, Ltd.
P.O. Box 64383
St. Paul, MN 55164-0383, U.S.A.

Table of Contents

Dedication
To Kate and Ken, with love.

Part I

THE FINDS

CHAPTER ONE

There's a mystery in South Africa. For years, miners in the Western Transvaal, near the little town of Ottosdal, have been finding metal spheres in a layer of Precambrian sediment. The spheres are of two types. One is a simple solid metal ball, bluish in color with flecks of white. The other is a hollow orb with a white spongy center. Many are about the size of a baseball, and the resemblance is heightened by three parallel grooves cut around one of them. Hundreds of these spheres have now been unearthed. They look manmade, but their location indicated they must be at least 2.8 billion years old.

Professor A. Bisschoff, a noted geologist at the University of Potchefstroom, thinks they are limonite concretions, but there are several problems with this theory.

Limonite is a type of iron ore formed from the oxidation of other iron minerals. It is common in marshes and certain types of sedimentary rock, notably limestone. Paint makers know it as a source of ocher and umber pigments. It certainly has a tendency to form concretions (the geological term for hard, rocky masses which build up over time around a central nucleus), but limonite concretions are yellow, brown, or black, not blue with white flecks. You find them in groups, usually stuck together, not as single, isolated spheres. They have never before shown a grooving effect. They exhibit a hardness factor of 4 to 5.5 on the standard Mohs scale, which makes them relatively soft. The metal spheres are made of something so hard they can't be scratched by steel.

If not limonite, what then? According to Roelf Marx, curator of Klerksdorp Museum where several of the spheres are on display, they were found in a strata of pyrophyllite. Is it possible they are a concretion of this silicate mineral? Once again, the answer seems to be no. Silicate minerals form crystals under pressure, not metal balls. Pyrophyllite looks like talc and is used in much the same way. It can form granular masses, but these have a greasy feel and are pale

3

in color. The question of hardness is even more conclusive. The Mohs figures for pyrophyllite are 1 to 2. You can't get any softer.

If they are not natural formations, where did the spheres come from? They have the appearance of artifacts, balls manufactured in a factory from specially toughened steel for a specific purpose. Yet on the face of it, they can't be manmade.

According to the experts, the first appearance of modern humanity, *Homo sapiens sapiens*, occurred around 100,000 years ago in southern Africa. The place is right, but the time isn't and the level of development is entirely wrong. These first humans lived a hunter-gatherer existence. They used stone, bone, wood, but not metal. The manufacture of the simplest iron artifact was beyond them, let alone the possibility of smelting steel.

Even if we ignore the question of technical ability, it is impossible to get the timing right. The predecessors of modern humanity, *Homo erectus* (or Upright Man) were building their own shelters in the Olduvai Gorge 1.8 million years ago, long before the appearance of sapiens, but long after something dropped those spheres in Western Transvaal.

Even earlier ancestors, *Homo habilis* (or Handy Man), were making primitive stone tools (but not metal balls) somewhere between 2.5 and 3 million years ago—still far too late to account for the mystery finds. In fact, the spheres were in place when the very first hominids diverged from the apes somewhere between *five and eight million years ago!*

To put the age of the South African find in perspective, Precambrian time comprises that long period of geological history between the formation of the Earth 4.6 billion years ago, and the beginning of the Paleozoic era, about 600 million years ago. Fossil finds from the period are rare, but geologists have built up a rough picture of prevailing conditions.

First, the atmosphere was probably much like our own, a mix of nitrogen, carbon dioxide, water vapor, and oxygen. There were seas and continents, although their contours would be quite unrecognizable today. The world was dominated by what scientists call supercontinents, enormous primeval land masses which eventually broke apart to form the continents we know now.

There was life of a sort. What appear to be fossilized algae or bacteria have been found in South African rocks older than three billion years. This is confirmed by the presence of stromatolites, rock structures formed in shallow water under algae mats. There is no indication at all of animal life on land and even shell fossils —indicating the sort of sea life we might recognize—are virtually nonexistent. The most advanced traces geologists can come up with are of soft-bodied multicellular organisms officially classified as animals, but standing on the evolutionary ladder somewhat lower than a jellyfish. It is obvious that no living creature of Precambrian times could have manufactured the Transvaal spheres.

These are not the only odd artifacts that require an explanation. Maximilien Melleville, vice president of the Société Académique of Laon, France, reported in *The Geologist* of April 1862 the discovery of a perfectly formed chalk ball in an early Eocene lignite bed near his home. The ball and its immediate surroundings showed evidence of having been carefully shaped from a larger block, then freed by a sharp blow—manufactured, in other words. There was no question of its having been placed in the stratum at a later date. Melleville was quoted:

> "It ... is penetrated over four fifths of its height by a black bituminous color that merges towards the top into a yellow circle and which is evidently due to contact with the lignite in which it has for so long a time plunged... As to the rock in which it was found, I can affirm that it is perfectly virgin and presents no trace whatsoever of any ancient exploitation. The roof of the quarry (where the ball was found) was equally intact in this place and one could see there neither fissure nor any other cavity by which we might suppose this ball could have dropped down from above."

Here again it would seem we are looking at a manmade artifact, but the placing of the ball in the lignite stratum assigns it an age between forty-five and fifty-five million years, well before the appearance of humanity on the planet.

An even greater mystery surrounds the report of a much more recent find. In 1928, a miner named Atlas Almon Mathis was working at depth in a mine two miles north of Heavener, Oklahoma, when blasting operations unearthed some twelve-inch cubical polished blocks which proved to be made from a type of concrete. A cave-in subsequently revealed the blocks had apparently been part of a wall which seemed to run more than 150 yards. The fact they were found in a coal seam means, in that area, they were at least 286 million years old. The obvious question is, who built the wall?

Perhaps the same persons who dropped the gold chain "of quaint and antique workmanship" into what became a coal seam of the Taylorville or Pana mines in southern Illinois. It was discovered by Mrs. S. W. Culp when she broke open a piece of coal preparatory to burning it on her fire.

There are several other impossible artifacts from the same era. A coal mine in Wilburton, Oklahoma produced a barrel-shaped block of solid silver "with the prints of the staves on it" according to a contemporary source. The same mine produced an iron pot. While Frank J. Kenwood was working with the Municipal Electric Plant at Thomas, Oklahoma in 1912, he used a sledge hammer on a piece of coal too large to use. The piece split and, witnessed by a fellow employee, the pot fell out.

Even odder was the carved stone found in the Carboniferous strata of a mine near Webster City, Iowa. According to a report in the Daily News of Omaha, Nebraska:

"Over the surface of the stone, which is very hard, lines are drawn at angles, forming perfect diamonds. The center of each diamond is a fairly good face of an old man having a peculiar indentation in the forehead that appears in each of the pictures, all of them being remarkably alike. Of all the faces, all but two are looking to the right."[1]

In June of 1884 the London Times reported the find of a length of gold thread imbedded in stone at a rock quarry close to the river Tweed. All these reported finds are at least 260 million years old. The gold thread may be as old as 360 million.

The founder of the British Association for the Advancement of Science, physicist Sir David Brewster, lends the weight of his reputation to a report in 1844 that a metal nail was found at Kingoodie Quarry in Scotland, embedded in a block of sandstone dating to the Devonian era , some 360 to 408 million years ago. The head of the nail was completely encased in the stone, ruling out any possibility that it had been driven in after the stone was formed.

Older still was the relic discovered in June 1852, at Dorchester, Massachusetts. A report in *Scientific American* described how blasting operations at Meeting House Hill produced two halves of a metallic vessel blown from the solid rock. According to the report:

"On putting the two parts together, it formed a bell-shaped vessel 4.5 inches high, 6.5 inches at the base and 2.5 inches at the top and about an eighth of an inch in thickness. The body of this vessel resembles zinc in color or a composition metal in which there is a considerable portion of silver. On the side there are six figures or a flower or bouquet beautifully inlaid with pure silver and around the lower part of the vessel a vine or wreath also inlaid with silver. The chasing, carving and inlaying are exquisitely done by the art of some cunning workman."[2]

There were no workmen about to make this exquisitely decorated vase, however. From its origins in the stone, we have to assume it to be greater than 600 million years old.

Endnotes

1. "Carved Stone Buried in a Mine." *Daily News*, Omaha, Nebraska. April 2, 1897.

2. "A Relic of a Bygone Age." *Scientific American*. June 5, 1852.

CHAPTER TWO

There are only two possible explanations for the sort of finds we have been examining. One is that they were weird natural formations. This is what Professor A. Bisschoff argued in respect of the Transvaal spheres. A similar explanation was attempted in relation to the chalk ball from France, but how could items like the metal nail, the pot, and especially the intricately decorated vase have been the result of purely natural processes?

If they were not natural formations, they must have been manufactured somewhere and by someone—or something—with intelligence. Is it possible we are looking at the first real evidence of extraterrestrial life?

Three conditions are important when considering the possibility of life on other planets: temperature, water, and atmosphere. Although these conditions need not be exactly the same as Earth, scientists have set the limits beyond which life, as we know it, simply could not exist.[1] These limits are bounded by what is called an *ecosphere*. The ecosphere for any given star is defined as the (usually small) range of distances from the star where any planets might have temperatures suitable for life, water in liquid form, and an atmosphere that did not boil off into space.

The ecosphere of our Sun includes the Earth, Moon, and Mars, but investigation of these last two shows that even in the ecosphere, there is no guarantee of suitable conditions for life. The Moon lacks both atmosphere and water. Its temperature range varies between 117 degrees Celsius (240 degrees Fahrenheit) and -190 degrees Celsius (-310 degrees Fahrenheit). Mars is a little more promising. There are suspicions of water locked in the form of ice at the polar cap. Temperatures at the equator of 17 degrees Celsius (62 degrees Fahrenheit) would be pleasant for a human visitor, but the atmosphere is pure carbon dioxide with a pressure of only 6 millibars. (Our own atmospheric pressure is over 1,000 millibars at sea level.) Some evidence of microscopic organisms having been on the planet at one time has recently surfaced, but most scientists assure us intelligent Martians exist only in the pages of fiction.

Once you go outside the ecosphere, the inner planets Mercury and Venus are far too hot to sustain life, while the outer planets are far too cold. If there is any other candidate for life in our solar system, it would have to be Io, the third-closest satellite of the planet Jupiter and the most volcanically active solid body known. Photographs taken by the Voyager I spacecraft in 1979 show a 2,259-mile diameter body (about a quarter the size of Earth) that appears yellow, red, brown, black, and white. Its surface temperature has been measured at -148 degrees Celsius (-235 degrees Fahrenheit), but a 27 degrees Celsius (80 degrees Fahrenheit) temperature was recorded by Voyager near a volcanic plume. This led to speculation about the possibility of limited organic life, but most scientists don't believe it, and no scientist imagines such life could be any more highly evolved than algae. Wherever the Transvaal spheres came from, it wasn't Io.

If we look beyond the solar system, however, the picture changes. There are so many stars in the universe that the probability of life elsewhere approaches certainty. It is even certain that some of this life must be intelligent, but if you are searching for visitors with a cargo of metallic spheres, the question of distance comes into play.

The fastest mover in the universe is light, which has a speed of 186,000 miles (299,792 km) per second. Einstein showed the speed of light is an absolute—nothing can exceed it. The astronomical measure of a light-year is the distance light travels in a vacuum in one year—some 9.46 trillion kilometers. Our closest star, Alpha Centauri, is 4.3 light-years away.

What all this means is that any extraterrestrial tourist visiting Earth will almost certainly originate within our own galaxy. Anywhere else is just too far. What are the probabilities of a space-faring civilization within the Milky Way?

One attempt to assess the various factors involved was made by the radio astronomer Frank Drake with his famous Green Bank Formula: $N = R^* f_p n_e f_l f_i f_c L$.

This daunting equation expresses the number of technical civilizations in the Milky Way Galaxy in terms of the factors necessary to sustain intelligent life. The first three of these factors are physical: the rate at which stars form, the fraction of those stars that have planets, and the average number of planets per star capable of supporting life.

The next two factors are biological: the fraction of those planets on which life actually arises and the fraction of planets where the life is intelligent. The final two factors are social. They represent the fraction of intelligent life planets that evolve technical civilizations capable of interstellar communication and the average lifetime of such civilizations.

Each of these factors is very difficult to quantify. There is good reason to suppose the average rate of star formation in our galaxy is ten, but beyond that we plunge deeper and deeper into guesswork. No planets have ever been detected with certainty outside our solar system. Orbital variations in about half our closest stars may be made by planets, but even if this was absolutely established, we have no way of knowing whether it is a general rule throughout the galaxy.

The question of life's origins is equally uncertain. In 1953, the American biochemist Stanley Lloyd Miller showed that if hydrogen, ammonia, methane, and water vapor were subject to radiation, organic molecules would be produced. Later experiments showed that components of DNA and RNA, the basis of life on Earth, could also be produced in this way. Organic molecules have since been discovered floating freely in space, but how they might evolve into life is not actually known.

When we come to the question of technical evolution, the problem deepens. The only known example of a technical civilization is our own. The estimate of time taken to develop such a technology depends on how you define the beginnings of technology—the discovery of fire? the invention of the wheel? the development of the cuckoo clock?—another way of saying it depends on the individual scientist's prejudices.

These uncertainties led scientists to assign best-guess values to the various factors. This resulted in their calculating that the number of technical civilizations in our galaxy stood around one—a discovery they might have made by looking through the window. Different values obviously produce different results, and some scientists have fed in figures that placed the total of technical civilizations in the galaxy as high as ten million. Nobody pretends this is anything more than guesswork, but it has encouraged the establishment of SETI (Search for Extraterrestrial Intelligence) projects.

After centuries of ground-based studies with telescopes, the search for life in our solar system reached its highest point to date with the landing in 1976 of two Viking spacecraft on Mars. They contained experiments designed to look for the biological processes of metabolism, photosynthesis, and respiration. In the metabolism experiment, a Martian soil sample was covered with a nutrient containing radioactive carbon-14, on the assumption that any organisms in the soil would eat the nutrient and give off carbon-14 gas. Large amounts of the gas were indeed detected, but the then scientific consensus was that no life signs were present. In 1996, NASA scientists announced analysis of a Martian meteorite found in the Antarctic showed traces of fossil bacteria. This indicated primitive life forms existed on the planetary surface billions of years ago, but scientists strongly stressed that there was no evidence at all of advanced life, let alone intelligence.

The search for extraterrestrial intelligence outside the solar system is at present carried out with radio telescopes. The first attempt was made by Frank Drake in 1960 at the National Radio Astronomy Observatory in Green Bank, West Virginia. Drake's Project Ozma focused on the stars Epsilon Eridani and Tau Ceti.

Between 1960 and 1980, at least eight searches for extraterrestrial intelligence were carried out around the world, all of limited duration and all unsuccessful. Despite occasional excited claims to the contrary, this remains the situation up to the present day.

Just because we have not yet detected life outside of Earth is no reason to assume it isn't there, though; and if life is there today, it might well have been there 2.8 billion years ago. It is difficult to imagine why such life would have chosen to visit an obscure planet where the highest intelligence was a patch of algae, but it could have happened. It is possible, if only just, that alien creatures from the distant reaches of our galaxy landed in the Precambrian wilderness of South Africa and dropped the metal spheres.

But the 500 million-year-old footprint found in Utah belongs to a man.

Endnote

1. Science fiction writers have speculated about totally different life
    chemistries, but we have no proof at all that these are actually possible.

CHAPTER THREE

Trilobites are extinct marine creatures whose fossils date from about 600 million to 225 million years ago. They look a little like tiny lobsters and may be closely related to living crustaceans, spiders, and horseshoe crabs.

William J. Meister, a draftsman by profession, collects trilobite fossils as a hobby. In the summer of 1968, he split open a block of shale near Antelope Spring, Utah, hoping to add to his collection, and found a fossilized human shoe print. The heel was indented about an eighth of an inch more than the sole and had the characteristic signs of wear that would mark it as a right shoe.

On July 4, Meister brought Dr. Clarence Coombs of Columbia Union College, Tacoma, Maryland, and geologist Maurice Carlisle, University of Colorado at Boulder, to the site. Carlisle dug for two hours before finding a mud slab which convinced him the formation had at one time been on the surface, and was consequently suited to the preservation of genuine fossil tracks.

The problem was it had not been at the surface for a very long time. The shale, which held trilobite remains as well as the shoe print, came from Cambrian strata dated somewhere between 505 and 590 million years old.

This was too much for the scientific community to swallow. When Meister published news of his discovery, a Brigham Young University geologist stated flatly that the "track" was actually an oddity of weathering. A Michigan professor of evolutionary biology suggested it might be a case of willful misrepresentation or outright fabrication. "There is not one case where a juxtaposition of this type has ever been confirmed," he said.[1]

One reason why juxtapositions of the type have never been confirmed may be that scientists, like the professor, have been content to pronounce on them without actually examining the evidence. This may not be altogether surprising. Mr. Meister was unwise enough to announce his find in *Creation Research Society*

Quarterly, an anti-evolutionary publication that tends to irritate those few scientists who bother to read it.

The biologist and geologist William Lee Stokes, of the University of Utah, did take the trouble to examine the print itself, but concluded, with his less conscientious colleagues, that it could not be genuine.

The problem, he stated afterwards, was that "at the very least we would expect a true footprint to be one of a sequence showing right and left prints somewhat evenly spaced, of the same size and progressing regularly in one direction."[2] Stokes found it "most significant" that no other matching prints were obtained.

To a layperson, it might seem unreasonable to demand a whole series of well-preserved fossil prints from a time period dating back 500 million years, but Stokes claimed categorically that he knew of "no instance where a solitary one-of-a-kind impression has been accepted and reported in a scientific journal as a genuine footprint no matter how well preserved it might be."[3]

Science authors Michael A. Cremo and Richard L. Thompson have suggested he should have consulted the *Scientific American*.[4] This respected publication was quite prepared to accept and report a solitary one-of-a-kind fossilized hominid footprint found by Henry de Lumly at Terra Amata, Southern France, in 1969.

Thompson also took issue with Stokes' claim that "a true footprint should also show displacement or squeezing aside of the soft material into which the foot was pressed," and he could find no evidence of this from his examination of the fossil. Thompson, who examined the print himself, pointed out that any displacement would depend on both the nature of the object making the footprint and the consistency of the ground in which it was made.

"We have observed," he said, "that shoes and sandals can leave very sharp impressions in relatively compact, moist beach sand with very little sign of pushing aside of the matrix."[5]

The same, he suggested, might hold good for certain consistencies of clay, mud, or silt—the material from which the Cambrian shale was originally formed. This was especially so when one considered that the fossil under examination appeared to be a shoe-print as distinct from a footprint. The rounded contours of a naked foot push aside far more clay than the sharp edges of a shoe.

Cremo and Thompson carried out a computer analysis of the print and found it deviated in no way from the type of print that would be left by a modern shoe, but if the shoeprint is genuine, we can no longer fall back on the idea of extraterrestrial visitors in Earth's distant past. What we have is an indication that a representative of the human race was strolling through Utah 500 million years ago.

The reason scientists are so resistant to the idea is that it is, in evolutionary terms, preposterous. The current picture of human evolution insists that the evolutionary ancestors of modern man, known as hominids, diverged from those of the apes somewhere between five and eight million years ago.

Hominids evolved into early tool-making proto-humans *Homo habilis*, or Handy Man. Their fossil bones were discovered in 1964 at Olduvai gorge in Tanzania, East Africa, by the British anthropologist Louis Leakey and others. These fossils were distinguished from those of *Australopithecus*, another extinct hominid, by a number of physical attributes, including the presence of a larger brain case, smaller rear teeth, and skeletal bones that more closely resemble those of modern humans.

The exact position of *Homo habilis* in human evolution is still uncertain. Some scientists believe it to be the earliest member of our species, suggesting a long evolutionary history independent of *Australopithecus*. Others suggest it represents the evolutionary transition between the earlier australopithecine, *Australopithecus africanus*, and later members of the species *Homo erectus*, or Upright Man.

Whatever the exact sequence, scientists are confident erectus evolved into *Homo neanderthalis*, Neanderthal man, and *Homo sapiens sapiens*, our own species, about 100,000 years ago.

There may be room for some adjustment of this picture. It is possible to imagine that new finds may push back human evolution a few hundred thousand years, perhaps even a million or two, but there is absolutely no question of humanity having evolved on our planet during the Cambrian period. In fact, there is absolutely no question of humanity having evolved prior to sixty-five million years ago, for a very interesting reason.

The sixty-five million date represents a evolutionary watershed in that it marked the death of the dinosaurs. Science is not quite sure why they died off, only that they did in a remarkably short space of time. The currently fashionable theory is that a comet collided with the Earth causing climatic changes which, while temporary, nonetheless lasted long enough to ensure that the dinosaurs, which had dominated our planet for 185 million years, were obliterated.

It was this obliteration that created an evolutionary gap which an opportunist little species raced to fill. That species was the mammals, the now huge classification of animals to which humanity belongs. While there were dinosaurs on earth, mammals had little chance to develop. It was only after the dinosaurs had gone that the species began to evolve into its present diversity.

Sheep, goats, cows, horses, and humanity all owe their existence to a tiny, tree-dwelling, shrew-like creature that began to multiply in the aftermath of the hypothetical comet. Despite a few attempts by Hollywood to persuade us otherwise, humanity was never contemporary with the dinosaurs—the evolutionary foundation for humanity was not laid until the dinosaurs disappeared.

Is it then possible that our reliance on evolutionary theory might be unjustified? There is still a body of thought that maintains, with Scripture, that God made man distinct and separate from the animals. This theory has no problem with Jurassic Man, or Carboniferous Man, or even Precambrian Man, because humanity did not have to evolve out of anything. We were simply set down to rule a world filled up with other species.

Charles Darwin's publication, in 1859, of his master work *On the Origin of Species* caused a storm of controversy that embraced not only the religious but the scientific world of his day. The fossil record has consistently and increasingly supported his evolutionary theory. Computer models, like those developed by Richard Dawkins, have shown how the process works. As one professor put it testily, "I put the creationists[6] and those who believe in a flat earth in the same category. They simply do not want to believe in facts and hard evidence. Nothing has emerged in recent years to refute the fact that evolution has, and continues to occur." [7]

If the theory of evolution still holds up and humanity simply could not have evolved on this planet prior to sixty-five million years ago, then how do you explain the 500 million-year-old footprint? I can only think of one real possibility. The man who made it traveled back in time.

Endnotes

1. *Forbidden Archaeology*, Cremo and Thompson. Bhaktivedanta Institute, San Diego, 1993.

2. Ibid.

3. Ibid.

4. Ibid.

5. Ibid.

6. Those who believe in the special, separate creation of humanity.

7. *Forbidden Archaeology*, Cremo and Thompson. Bhaktivedanta Institute, San Diego, 1993.

Part II

THE PHYSICS

CHAPTER FOUR

Time travel has its problems. One of the most famous is the grandfather paradox. Simply stated, the grandfather paradox says that if you could travel through time, then it would be possible for you to murder your grandfather. But if you murdered your grandfather, then you would never have been born so you could not have traveled through time to murder your grandfather.

A variation on the grandfather paradox (which also cheerfully involves murder) is the Hitler paradox. In this one you travel back in time to murder Hitler before he starts the Second World War, thus saving millions of lives. But if you murder Hitler in, say, 1938, then the Second World War will never come about[1] and you will have no reason to travel back in time to murder Hitler!

Large numbers of people, many of them philosophers, some of them scientists, have resolved paradoxes like these by concluding time travel is impossible. Others aren't so sure. A resolution to the grandfather paradox which still allows for time travel says that you can travel back in time, but you can only murder your grandfather after he has sired your father. If you try to murder him before that critical event, the Laws of Time won't let you.

The problem with this resolution is that nobody knows what the Laws of Time actually are. Indeed, the paradoxes themselves are constructed on the unspoken premise that we know what time is, or at least know how it works.

This is a common-sense approach based on experience. We think of time as flowing like a river, from the past into the future. It is, in short, linear. Even physicists talk about the arrow of time, a phrase that conjures up a wonderful picture of time as flying straight and true from here to there.

It is quite chastening to discover this common-sense picture of time is relatively new. It was also, for much of its history, quite localized. Aristotle thought time was circular and, with the sole exceptions of the Hebrews and the Persians, every ancient people agreed with him. The Stoics linked circular time with astronomical observation and believed that when the constellations and planets returned to the same positions they had occupied at the beginning of time, the universe would be renewed. The same view is found in Hinduism, which believes the world and humanity travel through a series of ages, known as *yugas*, always returning to its beginnings like an eternally spinning wheel.

The idea itself came round again in the nineteenth century when the prominent scientist Henri Poincaré produced a theorem which indicated that, given enough time, any closed system will return to its initial state. If you have an unlimited amount of time at your disposal, then the system will return to its origins again and again, indefinitely. Since the universe itself is a closed system,[2] Poincaré's Return supports the Stoics and the Hindus.

The fourth-century Bishop Nemesius of Emesa made the concept personal. "Socrates and Plato and each individual man will live again, with the same friends and fellow citizens," he said. "They will go through the same experiences and the same activities. Every city, village and field will be restored, just as it was. And this restoration of the universe takes place not once, but over and over again—indeed to all eternity without end."[3]

A variation on the theme appeared in *Groundhog Day*, a movie where the hero, played by Bill Murray, almost went out of his mind because he was condemned to live the same day over and over again. Exactly the same idea was expressed by the philosopher P. D. Ouspensky who concluded life and time were a matter of eternal recurrence. You were born, say, in 1912, lived your Biblical three score and ten to die in 1982 ... at which point you were promptly reborn in 1912 to do it all over again, exactly as you had before. Ouspensky wrote a novel about it, *The Strange Life of Ivan Osokin*, in which the hero had the opportunity to exercise free will within the overall confines of recurring situations. But in his non-fiction works, he made it clear he believed it difficult, if not downright impossible, to deviate from the predetermined pattern.

Our mainstream Judeo-Christian tradition has no patience with this sort of Russian gloom. To us, time's arrow really does fly straight and true, never deviating one iota as it travels from the distant past into the distant future. We sail on time's river and once objects and actions fall into the past, they are lost and gone forever: "The moving finger writes, and having writ moves on," as Omar Khayyam succinctly put it, reflecting the tradition of his native Persia.

Sad though the loss of our past might be, linear time has its compensations. It allows for the concepts of progress, of free will, of forgive and forget. It allowed Darwin to speculate on the origins of species and the process of evolution—an impossibility if time was circular or if, as Ouspensky believed, we all rolled on the wheel of eternal recurrence.

The problem with common sense and experience is that they can sometimes lead us up the garden path. It is a matter of common sense that the sun goes round the earth: any fool can watch it happen on a cloudless day. Yet, the observation confounds us. The motion of the sun around the earth is an illusion caused by the rotation of our planet, a fact of life we do not experience directly and thus never absorbed into our common sense perceptions. The millions who once believed the earth was flat were not fools either. They were simply applying common sense and experience. Until the advent of flight, which allowed the curvature of the earth to be seen directly, it could only be inferred from logical deduction. Once again, common sense and experience led to inaccurate conclusions.

Could our common-sense view of time also be inaccurate? History has shown that when science investigates common-sense precepts, the reality behind them is often very different from the superficial appearance. What, then, has science got to say about the nature of time?

Sir Isaac Newton, the father of physics, came down on the side of common sense: "Absolute, true and mathematical time of itself and from its own nature flows equably and without relation to anything external." For him, if it was ten to three in London, it was also ten to three on Alpha Centauri, on the starship Enterprise, and everywhere else in the universe.

But his own mathematics betrayed him.

In all probability, you learned Newton's three laws of motion at school, as I did, and have by now forgotten the math behind them, as I have, but that math is remarkably interesting to any prospective time traveler.

The equation describing Newton's second law of motion links acceleration to the force applied—the harder you push it, the faster it goes. This means time appears twice in the equation, measuring both the rate of change in speed and the rate of change in position. You'll be relieved to hear I don't propose to go into the actual mathematics, which I find as difficult as you do. It is enough to mention that in the equation, the value for time is squared. That's the vital point, for it means that if you substitute negative time (i.e., time running backwards) for positive time, it makes absolutely no difference to the outcome. This is because multiplying a negative by a negative produces a positive result.

So Newton reduced the movements of celestial and other bodies to a series of mathematical laws which remain absolutely consistent whether time flows forward from the past to the future or backward from the future to the past. In other words, reversing the direction of time (which would seem to be fairly necessary if you have ambitions to become a time traveler) does not run contrary to any law of Newtonian physics.

This is a startling realization. It means, in essence, that we might imagine a world in which you rise as a corpse from your grave, throw off your burial clothes, and live a life backwards. You would grow younger and younger until you were sucked into your mother's womb, there to rest for nine months, getting smaller and smaller until the day you split in half to be absorbed into your mother's ovary and siphoned off by your father's penis. It's a bizarre thought, yet under the laws of Newtonian physics, it's not impossible.

But does it have anything to do with the real world? I know of no one who is living backward, and I doubt if you do either. Furthermore, the direction of time makes an enormous difference to the outcome of any process. Try unscrambling an egg or extracting the milk you just poured into your tea. A dropped plate smashes on the floor, but you will wait until hell freezes before the pieces rejoin themselves and jump back onto the counter-top.

All these commonplace experiences run contrary to the predictions of Newtonian physics, and while you and I may happily ignore that, scientists can't. The problem is that Newton's laws work, and work beautifully. We use them to design our motor cars and space rockets. We ignore them at our peril. So, when we come across things like scrambled eggs and broken plates that seem to contradict them, it is necessary to find an explanation.

Scientists have toyed with a number of explanations. One was that the smashed plate which reassembles itself is not actually impossible, just extremely rare. This was based on the realization that while there are infinite ways of breaking a plate, there is only one way of putting it back together again. Another was that dissipated energy (like the noise of the plate smashing) complicates the picture and produces one-way time without actually contradicting Newton's laws.

For one reason or another, both these theories—and a host of others—have proven unsatisfactory, but one potential explanation remained to intrigue scientists all the way to Einstein. This was the idea that time is not intrinsic to the physical universe at all, but is instead a function of the human mind. In other words, what we experience as time is nothing more than the way our mind orders events so that we can make sense of our experience.

I should mention that the organizing function of the human mind is very well established. Look through the window. You see trees, grass, fields, a stream, and so on. Or, if you live in a city, you see the urban environment of houses, offices, streets, and cars. In fact, you're not really seeing any of those things. What's happening is that light is reflected off different structures, hits your eye, and excites receptors in your retina. This triggers an electrical pulse along a nerve track which feeds information into your brain.

Your brain is being peppered by all sorts of information every second of every minute of your day. What your brain does is to organize that information so it makes sense to you. It does that by imposing patterns on the information—here is the pattern of a house, here is the pattern of grass and so on.

It is this organizing function which allows you to recognize a tree, even when you've never seen that particular species of tree before. You may not know the local pygmies call it the *ngoro-ngoro* tree, but you know it's a tree and not a cat. The organizing function inside your head makes sure of that.

The importance of the function is underlined by what happens in those rare instances when it breaks down. Neurologist Andrew Sachs described such an instance in his book *The Man Who Thought His Wife Was a Hat*. When shown a glove, this unfortunate patient described it as a container with five appurtenances, but was unable to work out what it might be used for. On leaving, he seized his wife's head and tried to put it on, suspecting by association that it might be his hat, but unable to organize his perceptions sufficiently well to realize it was nothing of the sort.

By invoking the organizing function of the human mind, scientists began to wonder if objective time was an illusion, no more than an aspect of human psychology. There were quite a few good reasons for suspecting this might be true, but the theory had some tricky implications.

One was that if time was an aspect of mind, then time must be susceptible to mental control and that, surely, must mean your mind, if not your body, should be capable of time travel.

Endnotes

1. Or, if it does, at least it won't be Hitler who caused it.

2. At least we think it is.

3. *The Arrow of Time*, Coveny and Highfield, Flamingo Books, Harper Collins, London, 1990.

CHAPTER FIVE

Some years ago while under medical treatment, I was lying heavily sedated on a couch in my doctor's office when a nurse walked in. I watched with growing delight as she crossed the room in a series of disjointed stages all of which, to my drugged perception, took place outside of time.

It was my second such experience. My first was far less respectable. As a child of the Sixties, I could hardly wait to smoke pot and eventually got hold of some that had been treated with a much more potent psychedelic. The result was an experience during which space distorted, light values changed, paranoia gripped me and, at one glorious point, I moved outside time and into eternity. Eternity surprised me. Until that moment I had thought of it (when I thought of it at all) as time stretching endlessly, but it was nothing like that. It was rather the *absence* of time.

It did not occur to me that either of these experiences was anything more than a drug-induced illusion. Nor would I argue the point today, but they are relevant to the idea that time is a matter of perception rather than a reality of the external world. In a sense, drugs do alter time, as do circumstances. Einstein is credited with the remark that when you sit on a red-hot stove, a minute seems like an hour, but when you sit with a pretty girl on a park bench, an hour seems like a minute. Those of us who have avoided red-hot stoves may nonetheless recall how a minute seemed like an hour while listening to a boring lecture.

The critical word is *seemed*. There is no way of showing that drugs or emotional states actually influence the flow of time in any significantly real way, whatever our subjective impression. We can only say that common experience—time flies when you're having fun—would tend to support the theory of time as an aspect of the mind. We have to go a great deal further to prove it.

In 1935, Dr. J. B. Rhine laid the first foundations of such proof when he and psychologist William McDougall founded the Duke

University Parapsychology Laboratory in North Carolina. Neither man was concerned with the nature of time. Rather, they were interested in an exploration of certain weird talents suspected to reside in the human mind and loosely grouped under the heading of ESP or extrasensory perception.

Extrasensory perception is defined as the ability to perceive objects, places, thoughts, or events without using any of the familiar sensory channels. Rhine's genius lay in his attempt to subject ESP to hard statistical analysis. He built his experiments on earlier attempts by psychical researcher Charles Richet to use cards in the study of thought transference and clairvoyance. Rhine employed a target deck of twenty-five cards in which five different symbols—a circle, a cross, wavy lines, a square, and a star—were repeated five times. If the deck (known as a Zener pack) was well shuffled and hidden from a subject, he or she should, on average, guess five correct cards in one runthrough. But some of Rhine's subjects consistently achieved averages of six to ten correct guesses per run. Because the probabilities of such scores were extremely low, Rhine and his associates concluded that they had demonstrated the existence of paranormal perception.

None of this is at all relevant to our present theme, but as the work continued and more scientists duplicated Rhine's experiments, it was noticed some subjects failed to guess the card mentally "sent" by the experimenter, but had a statistically significant pattern of guessing the *next* card to be drawn from the pack. In other words, they were predicting the future.

The fact that it was only a second or two in the future (the time it took the experimenter to move from one card to the next) has obscured the implications of these findings. Simply stated, the reality of precognition requires a new look at the nature of time. If it is possible to foresee the future, even by a second or two, it means that the future is somehow there to be seen. Thus, it is not time that flows like a river carrying us along from a disappearing past into a constantly created future. Rather, it seems we are the ones who "flow," examining events on our timeline as we go. In short, it suggests there might be something in the idea of time as a function of human perception.

One objection here is that while precognition is now a well-established fact of parapsychology, its appearance in the laboratory remains rare — far more so than, for example, telepathy. From this it might be argued that the statistical results produced by Rhine are the result of a freakish talent, which has far more to do with the nature of the mind than the nature of time. Surely, if time were really no more than the way we order experience, wouldn't there be far more instances of precognition?

Disturbingly, it appears there really are far more instances of precognition than is commonly realized. So many, in fact, that the phenomenon may be almost universal. The reason we are largely unaware of this is that most precognition occurs in dreams.

The idea that dream precognition might be commonplace was put forward in 1925, a year that marked the publication of something playwright J. B. Priestley described as "One of the most fascinating, the most curious and perhaps the most important books of this age." The work in question was *An Experiment with Time*, by a British engineer named J. W. Dunne. After a rather rambling beginning in which he discussed, among other things, animism, visualization, and alarm clocks, Dunne came to the point in Chapter Six with the following story:

> "In January, 1901, I was at Alassio, on the Italian Riviera, having been invalided home from the Boer War. I dreamed one night that I was at a place which I took to be Fashoda, a little way up the Nile from Khartoum. The dream was a perfectly ordinary one and by no means vivid, except in one particular. This was the sudden appearance of three men coming from the south. They were marvellously ragged, dressed in khaki faded to the color of sackcloth and their faces under their dusty sun helmets were burned almost black. They looked, in fact, exactly like soldiers of the column with which I had lately been trekking in South Africa and such I took them to be. I was puzzled as to why they should have traveled all the way from that country to the Sudan and I questioned them on that point. They assured me, however, that this was precisely what they had done. 'We have come right through from the

Cape,' said one. Another added: 'I've had an awful time. I nearly died of yellow fever.'

At that time we were receiving the *Daily Telegraph* regularly from England. On opening this paper at breakfast, the morning after the dream, my eye was caught by the following flaring headlines:

THE CAPE TO CAIRO
'DAILY TELEGRAPH'
EXPEDITION AT KHARTOUM"

Just over a year later, Dunne became aware of a second precognitive dream. This one was about the eruption of a volcano in Martinique which swept away the town of St. Pierre at a cost of 4,000 lives. At the time of the dream, Dunne was camping with the Sixth Mounted Infantry in a remote area of the then Orange Free State. When the next batch of newspapers arrived, the Daily Telegraph confirmed the details of his dream, with one notable exception. Dunne had been convinced the death toll numbered 4,000. The *Telegraph* gave it as 40,000. It was this discrepancy that gave Dunne his first clue to what was going on because, in his excitement, he misread the newspaper figure and believed for fifteen years his total of 4,000 had been confirmed. This suggested his dreams did not foreshadow the actual event, but rather his reading of the newspaper account that described it.[1]

Wisely, Dunne realized he was not dealing with spirit messages, psychism, or anything of that sort, but rather a hitherto unsuspected anomaly in the structure of time. He realized that for most people, most dreams are simply forgotten and speculated that the familiar sensation of *déjà vu* might be triggered by an otherwise forgotten precognitive dream. He found himself drawn to the following speculation:

"That dreams—dreams in general, all dreams, everybody's dreams —were composed of images of past experience and images of future experience blended together in approximately equal proportions. That the universe was, after all, really stretched out in Time, and that the lop-sided view we had of it—a view with the "future" part unaccountably missing, cut off from the growing "past" part by a traveling "present moment"—was due to a purely mentally imposed barrier which existed only when we were awake.

To test this speculation, he proposed the "experiment with time" from which he drew the title of his book. Readers were encouraged to record their own dreams—notably those which occurred before a change in routine, such as a journey—and analyze them for images drawn from their immediate future.

Dunne's book was received with such interest that it became a bestseller. John Buchan wrote a novel inspired by it, and a great many intellectuals took up the famous experiment. In later editions, Dunne included some results of other people's work in the field and in one case calculated the probabilities in favor of a temporal anomaly at 320,000 to one.

Dunne's insight into the structure of dreams stands up to rigorous examination. Toward the end of his life, the psychologist Carl Jung also suggested that the deepest layers of the unconscious function independently of the laws of space, time, and causality, giving rise to paranormal phenomena like precognition. I polled a number of professional psychoanalysts, whose work involves the constant examination of patients' dreams, and found without exception they accepted the precognitive aspect of dreams as a matter of course. The same structure is evident in my own dream record, kept daily over a period of several years.

The phenomenon is, as Dunne suggested, open to personal investigation by anyone who cares to try it. The trick is to remember that you are not searching for spectacular premonitions of world-shattering events—these will be obvious enough if they do arise—but rather for images drawn from future experience that your unconscious mind weaves into the dream fantasy. Some experience of orthodox dream analysis could be useful since the dreaming mind presents the evidence in symbolic form and it takes a little practice before one can tune in accurately. Dunne, for example, describes one case history in which the dreamer dreamed a group of people were throwing lighted cigarettes at his face. The waking incident that triggered this image was a shower of sparks caused by a circular saw striking a nail. Psychoanalysts are well accustomed to teasing out this sort of symbolism from a patient's past. In Dunne's experiment it is necessary to tease it out from the future.

Dunne used the results of his experiment to construct a theory of serial time in which observers watched observers in an infinite regress. The concept of serial observers made some sense, but the scientific community shied away from the infinite regress. Experience has shown that when any value in your equation reaches infinity, there is usually something wrong with your theory. Scientists, in particular physicists, can live with infinite values, as in the calculations pertaining to the singularity of a Black Hole, but only uncomfortably. You must provide them with rock-solid evidence before they will even contemplate the possibility, and this Dunne failed to do. His experiment remains to intrigue, but his concept of serial time has never really been taken seriously.

Oddly enough, there is a wholly different concept of time which would seem to fit Dunne's findings just as well and which is taken seriously in many quarters. This is the idea of time as a fourth dimension.

Endnote

1. He abandoned another possibility—that he was somehow in telepathic contact with the journalists who wrote the story—after a mounting body of evidence convinced him this could not be the case.

CHAPTER SIX

We are all familiar with the three dimensions of space: length, breadth, and height. But philosophers and, more recently, scientists have speculated on the possibility that time is actually a fourth spatial dimension. According to this view, ideas of birth and death are largely illusory. If you could somehow view yourself from the outside, you would see a massive worm-like creature, tapered to a baby at one end, decaying at the other and meandering through three dimensions of space even as it extends through the fourth.

It is possible to get an even clearer picture by studying a time-lapse photograph of a sprint race. What you see is a series of blurring images of the athlete stretched from the starting line to the finishing tape. Any one of the images represents the three-dimensional athlete, frozen, so to speak, in the act of running, but the whole of the picture represents his extension in time.

If time really is a fourth dimension of space, you can easily see how Rhine's predictive card-calling and Dunne's predictive dreaming could work. From a four-dimensional perspective, each of us is a complete being, already extended into areas of space we normally think of as future experiences. A few months ago, I was in London speaking at a seminar but in a sense I was already in London, already at that seminar, from the day I was born, because my four-dimensional body had a temporal extension which took me there.

This is not, of course, how I experience my life any more than it is how you experience yours. We cannot directly sense our temporal extension, but instead are conscious only of growing into it. Our consciousness sits on the leading edge of this growth which we think of as the present moment. It is the focus of our consciousness that creates the sensation of time passing, rather as looking through the window of a train creates the sensation of scenery passing, although we know the world outside the train is in fact standing still.

It may be that the subjective impression of growing into our temporal extension is not entirely an illusion. We are born with only limited extensions in three-dimensional space and grow to full size somewhere around puberty. Perhaps we begin with limited temporal extension as well. Perhaps it is the experience of growing into our temporal extension that conditions us to believe in a traveling consciousness hanging on the leading edge of evolving time.

Perhaps that conditioning breaks down occasionally, allowing our consciousness to flicker forward along our temporal extension just long enough to guess the next card in the Zener deck or read tomorrow's newspaper.

This form of time travel would actually be a memory function. We are all perfectly familiar with projecting consciousness backwards along our own time track to recall the pleasures and pains of yesterday. It is even known, through experiments with hypnosis and the electrical stimulation of the brain, that nothing is ever forgotten, although retrieval of the information can be difficult. In other words, our mind has access to the whole of our backwards time track, exactly as one would expect from the theory of four-dimensional space.

The difficulty is that we do not seem to have total access to the forward time track. The very best of subjects manage to score only a little over the odds in precognitive card tests. Even Dunne's dreamers snatch no more than an occasional image from the future. Compared with our past, our temporal extension forward hardly impinges on our consciousness at all.

All the same, this may be largely a matter of belief. Convince yourself that something is impossible and it becomes impossible. This is especially true of psychological processes. If you have never seen the future, perhaps that is because you are certain precognition is impossible and so you have never tried.

There is some evidence for this viewpoint. Parapsychologists sometimes divide their subjects into sheep who believe in ESP and goats who don't. Tests have shown consistently that sheep exhibit more positive signs of ESP than goats.[1] It is also true to say that specialists in predicting the future (such as tribal shamans) are rather better at it than the rest of us. Shamanic training involves substantial mental gymnastics and, sometimes, the use of powerfully psychoactive drugs. Furthermore, the shaman is initiated into a belief system that holds foreknowledge to be his prerogative. These are factors which would all tend to break down a conditioned response.

So, four-dimensional space could explain why we sometimes catch a glimpse of the future and have, by and large, little difficulty in remembering the past. It is simply a matter of attention. In normal circumstances our consciousness is located at a particular point in our temporal extension, traveling forward. When we pay attention to that part of the extension which trails behind us, we have an awareness of the past. But we are like runners with our eyes closed, so we are not at all aware of the temporal extension stretching ahead. Only in exceptional circumstances will our eyes open long enough to give us an intriguing glimpse.

What the concept of four-dimensional space cannot explain is the apparent ability of certain people to look beyond their own temporal extension.

In 1992, I published a book called *Nostradamus: Visions of the Future*[2] which dealt, as the title suggests, with the life and prophecies of the famous sixteenth-century French seer. Many of the Nostradamus quatrains—four-line verses in which he sought to predict the future—are controversial, but a few are so clearly predictive it is difficult to ignore their implications. Among the most important of them are the verses which deal with the French Revolution.

The French Revolution began in 1789 and took ten years to complete. The first suggestion that Nostradamus genuinely foresaw it is contained in a rambling letter to Henry II, published in 1555:

"Then there will be the commencement that will comprehend in itself what will long endure and in its first year there shall be a great persecution of the Christian Church, fiercer than that in Africa and this will burst out during the year one thousand seven hundred and ninety-two they will think it to be a renovation of time."

The Revolution did indeed mark a great persecution of the Christian Church, but it is the linking of the year 1792 with a revolution in time that is really impressive—1792 was the year the revolutionary calendar was inaugurated in France.

This was only the beginning. Elsewhere in his letter to King Henry, Nostradamus states that the persecution of the clergy would last a little less than eleven years. If we take the earliest beginnings of the persecution as July 12, 1790, the day the Civil Constitution was adopted, and assume that it ended with the Concordat of July 15, 1801, the actual period of persecution is eleven years and three days. This might seem a reasonable enough margin of error for a man viewing events from a distance of more than two hundred years, but in fact we need make no excuses. In 1792, the adoption of the Revolutionary Calendar caused the disappearance of nine days. When this is taken into account, it is clear that Nostradamus was absolutely correct in claiming the persecution would last "a little less than eleven years."

But it was in his quatrains that Nostradamus produced the most telling details of his predictions about the Revolution, and nowhere more clearly than his description of the "Flight to Varennes" of Louis XVI and his unpopular Queen Marie Antoinette.

By the year 1792, with the Revolution in full swing, Louis became convinced that he and his Queen were captive in their own country and became obsessed with the idea of escape. He decreed that their route should be through Varennes. Nostradamus, writing 230 years in advance of the event, predicted:

> *By night there will come by way of the forest of Reins*
> *A married couple arriving by a circuitous route.*
> *One a Queen, stony white, the King in gray like a monk at Varennes,*
> *An elected ruler. It shall result in tempest, fire and bloody slicing.*
>
> Century 9, Quatrain 20

There is, according to historian James Laver, only one mistake in this quatrain: no "forest of Reins" appears on any map. The remainder, however, is all too accurate. Here we had a married couple, a King and Queen, who traveled to Varennes by a circuitous route. The Queen was dressed in a white gown while the King was dressed in gray. Louis was indeed an elected King, the first in history, since prior to the Revolution, kings were believed to rule by divine right.

It was dark by the time the King arrived at Varennes, only to find a relay of horses he had expected was missing. While the party looked for it—the horses had, in fact, been left at the other side of the town—a revolutionary named Drouet, who had been following since he recognized the King in another town, caught up with them and blocked the exit road by overturning a cart of furniture on a narrow bridge. He then alerted Monsieur Saulce, the Procurer of the Commune.

The King's party reached the center of the town where the horses of the great coach were seized and papers were demanded. These were quickly produced and found to be in order (as they had to be since they were signed by the King himself), but by now crowds were pouring into Varennes alerted by the news of the King's flight. Saulce insisted that the party remain the night, and Louis, with no real alternative, agreed. By morning, a messenger had arrived from the National Assembly. The King was ordered to return. Nostradamus matched these events with the following prediction:

> *The husband alone will receive the mitre*
> *Returning, conflict will sweep across the Tuileries*
> *By five hundred men a traitor will be given Narbonne's title*
> *And from Saulce we will have oil.*
>
> Century 9, Quatrain 34

The "husband alone" was Louis. Following his return from Varennes, the Tuileries palace was invaded by a mob which forced the King to wear the red cap of liberty, a headpiece which bears a striking resemblance to a bishop's mitre. History records a second invasion some two months later of exactly five hundred men. The Comte de Narbonne was the King's war minister, a title soon bestowed on a revolutionary. Saulce was the Procurer who stopped the King at Varennes. By trade he was a merchant and chandler. One of his staples was the sale of oil.

Many experts would claim that in quatrain after quatrain, Nostradamus remorselessly chronicled the events that followed the fatal flight, but even the limited material quoted here may be enough to convince an open-minded reader that Nostradamus managed somehow to peer more than two hundred years into the future.

The study of Nostradamus' prophecies has largely become the province of occultists, cranks, and religious fanatics mainly concerned with extracting information about our own future from his work. With the exception of James Laver, it is difficult to find a reputable historian who takes Nostradamus seriously. No scientist would dare admit even to having examined the evidence. This is a great pity, because if only one of Nostradamus' prophecies is proven genuine, it has far-reaching implications for our ideas about the nature of time. Specifically, it must mean the explanation of four-dimensional space just will not do.

Nostradamus was born in 1503 and died in 1556, giving him a temporal extension of fifty-three years. Viewed from the four-dimensional perspective, he was a fifty-three-year-long timeworm largely occupying the geographical area of France. If through natural ability or training he was able to free his consciousness to travel along his forward time-track, he should have been able to grasp memories of events that lay in his own future (which, in fact, he seems to have done), but four-dimensional theory gives us no mechanism by which he would be able to project his consciousness beyond the point at which his temporal extension ended—in practical terms, beyond the point of his death. Yet if we accept that Nostradamus foresaw the French Revolution, he somehow managed to project his consciousness a distance of more than 230 years.

Nostradamus was not the only prophet of the French Revolution, just the most famous. In 1625, the German psychic John Englebrecht found himself watching the storming of the Bastille some 154 years in the future, long after he would be dead. The ecclesiastic Pierre d'Ailly did even better. He managed to predict the French Revolution from the fourteenth century, as did his contemporary Pierre Turrel. It is important to realize that these latter two predictions specify the actual date of the Revolution and were written down in manuscripts which have survived to the present day. There was none of the obscurity which characterizes so many of the Nostradamus quatrains. Both d'Ailly and Turrel stated clearly what it was they were expecting.

Many less spectacular, but often more detailed, case studies of this sort of prediction are in the files of the Societies for Psychical

Research in Britain and America. One of them concerns the American Civil War soldier, John R. Davis.

Welsh-born Davis joined the Fifty-third Ohio Regiment of the Union army in the early 1860s. In August 1863, his commanding officer, Major E. C. Dawes, told him that the regiment had been ordered to Natchez, in Mississippi. Davis promptly told him of a dream in which he had seen the regiment disembarking not at Natchez, but at Memphis, Tennessee. He described in detail how this would take place.

The dream proved accurate, as Major Dawes later confirmed in a letter to the Society for Psychical Research. Indeed, it had many of the hallmarks of a Dunne-type dream prediction, except for one thing: Davis died on September 5 from wounds received at the Battle of Chicamauga, before the regiment moved out. The prediction he had made lay, like those of Nostradamus, d'Ailly, Turrel and the rest, outside of his own timeline. The concept of four-dimensional time does nothing to explain it.

Endnotes

1. This is not to say they exhibit more ESP. Goats will often unconsciously use ESP to produce negative scores—i.e., scores which fall statistically below those predicted by the laws of chance.

2. Published in 1993 by Aquarian Press, London.

CHAPTER SEVEN

Newtonian physics was once thought capable of explaining a Nostradamus-type prophecy. If you know the laws of motion (and Newton was convinced that he had worked them all out), you can predict the future of a moving object. All you need is knowledge of certain initial conditions. The more information you have to start with, the more accurate your predictions will be.

This situation creates a dreadful chain of logic. If the laws of nature determine the future of an event, then it is obvious that, given enough information, you could have predicted it in the past. Again, given enough information, you could also have predicted your prediction even earlier, and predicted that event earlier still. All of which leads inevitably to the conclusion that, had you had enough information at the moment the universe was created, you could have predicted any event at any period of its future history. In other words, everything would be absolutely predetermined.

In the Newtonian universe, events play themselves out like the cassette in your tape deck, unfolding in the only way they can. The cosmos is a great clockwork machine, blindly ticking away the centuries, and you and I are no more than tiny cogs within it. The choices we appear to make, our striving for a better life, our moral concerns, the fundamental concept of free will, are all an illusion. Such a universe permits Nostradamus to make predictions far beyond his own lifetime, but it is a sterile place to live, a cosmos without meaning.

Fortunately, we now know we do not live in a predetermined universe. Newton's laws of physics were eventually superseded. They work well enough in the universe of bicycles and billiard balls, but fray at the edges when you try to apply them to very large masses of matter, to speeds close to that of light and to the behavior of very small things like atoms and sub-atomic particles. The man who blew the whistle on Newtonian physics was Albert Einstein.

What caused him to do so was a paradox physicists had been struggling with since 1887 when two of their number, Edward

Morley and Albert Michelson, set up an experiment that proved, among other things, the speed of light remained the same however fast you were traveling when you measured it.

The paradox is simply enough stated. You know the speed of light is 299,792 km or 186,000 miles per second. Set up a photographer's flash gun at one end of a racetrack then stand perfectly still at the other. When the flash goes off, you know the light is rushing towards you at exactly 299,792 km per second. Suppose you weren't standing still. Suppose you were astride a miraculous 1,200 cc Norton capable of traveling at 100,000 km per second. It is fairly obvious that if you ride your Norton towards the flash the light will reach you sooner than it would if you were standing still, and if you raced away from the flash, it would take the light that little bit longer to catch up. Effectively, your Norton would increase the speed of light to 399,792 km if you were riding towards it and decrease its speed to 199,792 if you were racing away.

That's common sense and Newtonian physics, but it's also just plain wrong. When Morley and Michelson carried out their famous experiment (appropriately known as the Morley-Michelson Experiment) they discovered that however fast your Norton travels in either direction, light still reaches you at exactly the same time. It doesn't make sense, but it's what happens.

This discovery upset physicists enormously, but there wasn't anything they could do about it. They struggled with the paradox for eighteen years until 1905 when Albert Einstein published his Special Theory of Relativity. In it, Einstein didn't so much resolve the paradox as swallow it whole. Instead of worrying about how the light could reach you simultaneously whichever way you rode your Norton, he started with the proven fact that it did. In other words, he started with the certainty, established by experiment, that the speed of light is constant.

Having gotten rid of that little problem for the moment, Einstein went on to borrow the theory of relativity. Most people imagine he invented it, but the credit for that has to go to the famous seventeenth-century astronomer, Galileo Galilei. Five years before he built his first telescope, Galileo was concerned with the physics of moving objects. Legend has it he dropped things of un-equal weight from the Leaning Tower of Pisa. His observations convinced him that the laws which govern falling bodies are con-sistent only when the frames of reference you are considering happen themselves to be moving uniformly in relation to each other. If you can understand that, you understand the world's first Theory of Relativity.

Einstein's Theory of Relativity (actually Theories of Relativ-ity since he published two) are a bit more complicated. He ex-tended Galileo's idea beyond the laws of motion to include all the laws of physics. So, Einstein's Special Theory of Relativity is built on two principles. The first is that the laws of nature are exactly the same providing your frames of reference are moving uniform-ly relative to one another. The second is that the speed of light re-mains the same in all frames of reference that move uniformly in relation to each other. If you understand those, you understand the Special Theory of Relativity.

You may not immediately grasp its implications, however, be-cause the implications of the second principle—that the speed of light is constant—are an absolute nightmare.

To discover the speed of anything, you need to measure the time it takes and the distance it covers. In other words, you need the equivalent of a clock and a ruler. But when you use your clock and ruler to measure the speed of light, you find it is always the same whether you are moving away from the source, moving to-wards the source, or standing still—that's to say, across three dif-ferent frames of reference.

Now, this is where things get hairy. If the speed of light doesn't change across these frames of reference, then your measuring in-struments must. It's impossible, but it's the only thing that makes sense. Einstein argued that a constant speed of light can only be the result of rulers growing shorter and clocks running slower if they happen to be moving.

Let's put that into context. You, your clock, and your ruler are all together in a moving frame of reference—a train, a plane, or a flying saucer: it doesn't matter so long as it's moving. Meanwhile, I am standing on the ground with my clock and ruler and we're both about to measure the speed of light. We both do so and sometime later compare our calculations. Since I'm an old-fashioned sort, I tell you my measurement came out at 186,000 miles per second. You tell me yours came out at 299,792 kilometers per second. When we make the metric conversion, we discover we've both got exactly the same result, which is, of course, impossible. (Ask any nineteenth-century physicist.) After a while, it occurs to us that getting into motion did something to your clock and ruler. Specifically, it made your ruler shorter, so the light had less distance to travel along it, and it made your clock run slower, so the light had more time to do so. The only reason you didn't notice this while you were in your flying saucer was that you were getting shorter and running slower at exactly the same rate.

What Einstein extracted from this Lewis Carroll scenario was that a moving object (any moving object, not just a ruler) contracts in its direction of motion and a moving clock runs more slowly than a clock at rest. What's more, the object gets shorter and the clock runs slower the faster they move. At the speed of light, the object gets so short it disappears altogether and the clock runs so slowly that it stops, but all this happens only from the viewpoint of the person standing still. Anybody moving right along with the clock and object would notice nothing unusual.

Before you grow too dazzled by disappearing objects and stopped clocks, I may as well mention there's an exciting little land mine hidden in there. Talking about clocks slowing and stopping brings to mind some sort of mechanical failure, as when grandfather's clock stopped short because the old man died. Einstein didn't mean that at all. What he meant was time slows when you get into motion and stops altogether when you reach the speed of light.

This is such an outlandish idea that you would want very solid proof before you thought to take it seriously. It is not, after all, the sort of thing you notice when you consult your watch on a bus. This is because buses simply move too slowly for the effect to be noticeable, but planes don't. In 1972, eight of the most accurate atomic clocks scientists could construct were carefully synchronized. Four of them were loaded onto an airplane, while the remaining four stayed firmly on the ground. The plane was then taken on a round-the-world flight. When it landed again, the clocks on the plane were running ever so slightly slower than their counterparts on the ground. The same experiment carried out on rockets produced the same result, proof positive that Einstein's theory worked in the real world.

It also works in the subatomic world. We know that certain little things called muons only live a very short time. We know this because we have managed to produce muons in the laboratory. Muons in the wild live seven times longer, because wild muons travel at ninety-nine percent the speed of light. The pion, another subatomic particle, shows a similar characteristic. Wild pions, which travel at eighty percent the speed of light, live 0.67 times longer than their lab counterparts, except that it isn't really a matter of living longer, as a wild lion might live longer than a zoo lion because it gets more exercise. It is actually a matter of time running slower for wild pions and muons because of the speeds they attain when they are manufactured in the sun.

The Space Shuttle rattles along at twenty-five times the speed of sound—about 26,550 km/h or 16,500 mph. So, outside of Star Trek, our fastest rockets come nowhere near the speed of light. If they did, we would be a long way towards constructing a time machine, but the problem is purely technical. We already know with absolute certainty what happens if you climb aboard a craft capable of carrying you at muon speed. This was worked out by Einstein in the form of his famous Twins Paradox.

In this scenario, you have a pair of identical twins, one of whom becomes an astronaut on a spaceship capable of approaching the speed of light. The astronaut takes off to boldly go where no astronaut has gone before, while his twin stays home to feed the cat.

Let's assume both twins were thirty years of age when the astronaut left. Let's also assume the space voyage is scheduled to last five years. On the ship, the astronaut twin ages five years according to every measure he can apply. So, by the time he gets home again, he's thirty-five years old: but remember the muon. This spaceship is traveling at ninety-nine percent the speed of light, so time is moving seven times slower on board than it is on the ground. That means the twin who stayed home has aged thirty-five years. He is now sixty-five years old and the cat is long dead. In other words, just because he raced at breakneck speed around the galaxy, the astronaut is now thirty years younger than his twin brother. You can see why this is called a paradox.

Science fiction writers have avoided this paradox by the simple expedient of denying twins the right to become astronauts. This permits the logical development of stories about starships which do better even than the muon and travel at 99.9 percent the speed of light. When they return home, the crew is still hale and hearty but centuries, even millennia, have passed on Earth. Fictional though they may be, such voyages are absolutely consistent with the laws of physics described in the Special Theory of Relativity, and they are, by any reasonable criterion, time travel.

It is time travel in one direction only, from the present to the future. There is no way the equations of the Special Theory of Relativity point to travel into the past. We move forward in time the way we always have.[1] Einstein's first thoughts simply mean there is no theoretical barrier against our moving forward in time a little faster and a little further than we do naturally. Leaping on the back of a horse enabled man to move faster and further in space than he could do unaided. Leaping into a near-light-speed spaceship enables him to do much the same thing in time.

Endnote

1. At least that's the assumption. Special Relativity, like Newtonian physics, does nothing to confirm time must necessarily flow in one direction. So, it's just as valid to say that the twin left on Earth grew younger relative to his astronaut sibling. What it isn't valid to say is that both grew younger or the spaceship managed to land before it ever took off.

CHAPTER EIGHT

It was Einstein's Special Theory of Relativity that gave us the concept of time as a fourth dimension of space. Hermann Minowski, Einstein's mathematics teacher, put forward the idea in 1908 after learning about his star pupil's theory. Einstein himself took the idea and ran with it—except he didn't actually put it the way Monowski had.

What he really said was that there was no such thing as (separate) space and time. There was only one single thing called space-time and it formed a continuum. A continuum is something that has parts, but they're stuck so close together you can't actually separate them. You may remember from your high school geometry that a line is comprised of an infinite number of points. The points are parts of the line, but they're stuck together so closely that you can't actually separate them. This means the line is a continuum.

If you were a one-dimensional being who came across a line sideways, you would not be aware of its extension at all. If you came upon it lengthways, you would be aware only of moving from point to point on an infinite journey. However you hacked it, you would never be aware of the line as a continuum, even though a continuum is definitely what it is. It's a bit like that when you consider space-time. You can deduce it must be a continuum, but you don't experience it that way. However you hack it, you still think of space as space and time as time.

Newton's belief was that there were three dimensions of space and everything in them moved forward through one dimension of time. We accepted that belief for centuries. Even now, when we know better, we still believe it because that's exactly how we experience space-time. Belief isn't enough to make something true, however. The reality of Special Relativity is that from a four-dimensional viewpoint everything past, present, and future already exists as a single fabric, a single continuum. That isn't the way we

49

experience it any more than the one-dimensional being experiences the line as a line, but that's the way it is.

Yet, the notion, which I advanced with such panache just a couple of chapters ago, that time is a fourth dimension of space, is not strictly accurate. It's certainly useful—it's already given us a clue to the way precognition may work—but it's only an approximation. Or, more accurately, it's a translation. The actual relationship between space and time can only really be expressed mathematically. In talking about time as a mysterious "direction" in a four-dimensional universe, I was trying to express in words what can properly be expressed only in mathematics. I knew I wouldn't get it exactly right, but I had to try because I'm not very good at mathematics.

Einstein once remarked that he wasn't very good at mathematics either. But he was fortunate enough to have Herman Minowski at hand, who was prepared to step in and do the hard work for him long after he left school. Three years after the publication of the Special Theory of Relativity, Minowski had calculated the mathematical ramifications of his former pupil's insights.

Those calculations were sheer poetry. They created a picture of space-time worthy of Shelley, Yeats, or Byron. It was a picture that showed mathematically the whole of your past and the whole of your future must meet, can meet, always and forever do meet at a single point. When you examine that point in the Minowski equations, you are looking at the eternal now of space-time. More exciting still, the calculations show the meeting point has a specific location. It can never be found other than at the precise position of the observer. All of your past, all of your future converges at the instant you read these words on the exact spot where you read them.

You can change your location in space without destroying the universe. The whole forwards/backwards convergence of your future and your past moves with you. But the real question is, can you change your location in time? Minowski nowhere suggests that you can, but if you do, his equations seem to indicate you must maintain your location in space. Interestingly, we have indications that on a surprisingly large number of occasions, for some extraordinarily lucky people, this has actually happened.

In 1912, at the age of 23, the historian Arnold Toynbee visited Greece. On January 10 of that year, he found himself perched on one of the twin summits of Pharsalus staring out over the sunlit landscape and thinking about the battle that took place in the vicinity in 197 B.C. Suddenly, he slipped into a time pocket (his words) and found himself back in the days when the forces of Philip of Macedon faced the Roman legions at this spot. The weather had changed. There was a heavy mist that parted to allow him a view of the downhill Macedonian charge that led to disaster. The Romans spotted a weakness in the Macedonian flank, wheeled their men and attacked with such ferocity that Toynbee had to turn his face away from the slaughter. Almost at once the scene disappeared and he was back in a peaceful, sunlit present.

Two months later it happened again, this time on Crete. He was at the ruins of a mountain villa when, with much the same sensation as an aircraft hitting an air pocket, he dropped into another time pocket. This one was rather more shallow than the 2,109-year pocket at Pharsalus. It extended just 250 years to the day when the house had abruptly been evacuated and abandoned.

Time slip happened to him again at Ephesus while he was inspecting the ruins of the open-air theater where St. Paul had his run-in with the local silversmith's guild. Acts 19 tells how a silversmith named Demetrius bemoaned the actions of Paul, who had been encouraging people not to buy temple statuary. The Biblical account continues in Demetrius' words:

> "So that not only this our craft is in danger to be set at nought but also that the temple of the great goddess Diana should be despised, and her magnificence should be destroyed, whom all Asia and the world worshippeth.
> And when they heard these sayings, they were full of wrath, and cried out, saying, 'Great is Diana of the Ephesians'."

Toynbee, it appears, saw it all. He was even able to pick out Paul's two companions Gaius and Aristarchus. As the chant of "Great is Diana of the Ephesians" died away, he emerged from this latest time pocket into his present day.

A month later, on April 23, he was back in another one. At this stage he was in Laconia and had climbed up to the citadel of Monemvasia. He clambered through a breach in the walls and came upon the remains of several bronze cannons in the undergrowth. At once he had the by-now familiar feeling of the air pocket and dropped back in time to 1715 when the citadel had fallen to the Turks.

The following month, he was at the ruins of Mistrà in Sparta watching the highland hordes from Màni lay waste to the citadel in 1821. The experience was so profound that it inspired him to write his monumental twelve-volume Study of History.

There was something about Toynbee that encouraged the slippage of time. A year before his trip abroad, he had found himself transported from Oxford to a back yard in the Teanum of 80 B.C., there to witness the suicide of an Italian Confederacy leader who had been betrayed by his wife. The slip was apparently triggered by reading of the incident.

Toynbee's multiple experiences—especially the last described—have a particular resonance for me since I went through something very similar in Ireland in 1973. I was living at the time in an eighteenth-century gate lodge at Dunboyne and researching a book I planned to write on Nazi Germany. To my delight, I had discovered an edited recording of the Nuremberg Trials. I switched on the recording, lay down on a couch, and pulled on a pair of padded headphones which cut out all extraneous sounds. I closed my eyes and listened to the voice of Joachim von Ribbentrop, the former Nazi Foreign Minister.

At once I was no longer in Ireland. The subjective impression was exactly as Toynbee described it: like dropping into an air pocket. With a jolt, I found I was watching and listening to the trial itself. I was actually able to determine the quality of the light and the predominant, rather dusty, smell of the room. The experience lasted only moments, then I was suddenly back in my home.

The key words in that paragraph are, of course, subjective impression. Although our entire experience of reality is a matter of subjective impression, there is no doubt but that our minds can pay all manner of tricks. Toynbee and I may have suffered from hallucinations or, put more kindly, visions or vivid fantasies.

Toynbee's prior knowledge of history would have given him the building blocks of any imaginary recreation. In my own case, the Nuremberg Trials experience was part of intensive, ongoing research into Nazi Germany.

All the same, while these experiences may certainly be fantasy, it is probably true to say we are only tempted to dismiss them because we believe time slips are impossible. You did not doubt, for example, the part of my account where I described playing the Nuremberg recording. This is because you are quite willing to believe (without necessarily having it proved) that sound recordings of the Nuremberg Trials exist.

There are other, similar accounts less easy to explain as creative fantasy. The author Stephen Jenkins tells of an incident near Mounts Bay in Cornwall during which he saw a horde of armed men in ancient clothing skulking in the bushes near the track where he was walking. He ran towards them, felt a sensation like passing through a curtain of warm air, then found the men had gone.

Frank L. Smythe describes how he entered a grassy hollow near Glen Glomach in the Scottish hills and experienced a time slip. He saw a small group of weary men, women, and children stagger into an ambush laid by men wielding spears, axes, and clubs. In the resultant massacre, every last member of the group was slaughtered. Smythe was so horrified he ran from the scene.

The interesting thing about this account—it happened in 1940—is that Smythe was a mountaineer, not an historian. He had no particular interest in or knowledge of the spot where the time slip occurred. He did do some research into the area, but only afterwards, as a result of his experience. On the debit side, Smythe was never able to confirm his experience. He discovered two massacres had happened at the spot, but the clothing and weaponry did not match with his vision.

Other cases, however, provide clear confirmation that experiences of this type can have a genuine historical reality. One drawn from my own files concerns a woman named Stella Knutt[1] who, in the late 1970s, was on a driving tour of the Wicklow Mountains in Ireland. She turned off onto a narrow road and drove past a solitary public house, then climbed until the road began to peter out.

Since it was obvious she would soon be unable to drive any further, she found a turning space and came back down again. As she reached the junction with the main road, she realized she had not passed the pub.

Although she suspected she had simply not been paying attention, she was sufficiently intrigued to turn and go back up the narrow road, this time specifically searching for the pub. She did not find it, but she did find the open space where it had been and the remains of its foundations and walls half-buried in the undergrowth.

In this case, there was no air-pocket sensation of dropping through time, but otherwise this description of a time slip has much in common with the others, particularly in its utterly real tone. (She recalled quite clearly seeing an old 1930s-style bicycle propped against the pub wall.)

P. J. Chase, of Wallington in Surrey, was also able to verify his time slip. He was waiting for a bus one afternoon in 1968 and decided to stroll a little way down the road to pass the time. This he managed to do in more ways than one. He came across two picturesque thatched cottages with hollyhocks in their gardens. One of them was dated 1837.

Next day Chase mentioned the cottages to a friend—only to be told they did not exist. He went to check and found the friend was right. The only buildings at the spot were two brick houses. When he made inquiries in the area, an elderly resident confirmed that the cottages had existed. They had been pulled down to make room for the houses some years previously.

The author Colin Wilson describes a time slip at Fotheringhay Church in Northamptonshire, the place where Mary Queen of Scots was executed.[2] For some time, the building had a reputation for being haunted and a number of people had reported hearing Elizabethan music coming from its interior when no one was inside. However, this was unknown to Mrs. Jane O'Neill, a Cambridge schoolteacher, when she visited the church in the early winter of 1973.

The visit seemed normal enough and she spent a good deal of time admiring a splendid picture of the Crucifixion behind the altar on the left side of the church. It had, she said, an arched top and within the arch was a dove with its wings following the curve of the arch.

Some hours later she was in her hotel room with a friend named Shirley, who was reading aloud from an essay which mentioned a particular type of arch.

"That sounds like the arch of the picture I saw in the church," Mrs. O'Neill remarked. But Shirley looked at her blankly. Although she had visited the church many times, she had never seen the picture.

Shirley's reaction worried Mrs. O'Neill. She (Mrs. O'Neill) had had a bad shock two months previously which left her with a tendency to see things. She rang the local postmistress, a woman who arranged flowers in the church every Sunday. The postmistress told her there was no picture of the Crucifixion, although there was a board behind the altar with a painting of a dove.

A year later, Jane O'Neill went back to Fotheringhay Church. The outside was exactly as she remembered it, but when she went inside she knew at once she was in a different building. It was much smaller than the Fotheringhay she had visited before. There was, as the postmistress had insisted, no painting of the Crucifixion. And even the dove behind the altar was totally different than the one she had seen.

Thoroughly disturbed by now, Mrs. O'Neill got in touch with a Northamptonshire historian, who told her that the original Fotheringhay Church had been pulled down in 1553 and the present building erected on the site. Further research soon confirmed that the church Mrs. O'Neill had entered in 1973 was the one that had been demolished more than four hundred years previously.

Endnotes

1. The name has been changed to protect the woman's privacy.

2. In his book *Beyond the Occult*, Bantam Press, London, 1988.

CHAPTER NINE

Every case study in the previous chapter conforms with the Minowski equations in that they involve (or appear to involve) a slippage in time, but not in space. When Mrs. O'Neill entered Fotheringhay church, she traveled to the sixteenth century, but remained in exactly the same spatial location. The same thing happened to Jenkins, Smythe, and the rest. Indeed, I can only find one convincing record of a time slip which may have involved a slip in space as well—although this is by no means certain. The facts of the case are as follows:

The biologist Ivan Sanderson spent some time with his wife in Haiti, conducting a biological survey. They were out with their assistant, Fred Allsop, when their car became bogged down in the mud in a remote area of the island and they were forced to walk home. Allsop went up ahead. Sanderson was walking with his wife when, to his astonishment, he saw a number of three-storied houses of varying types along both sides of the road. It was night, but he saw them quite clearly in bright moonlight, even noting that they cast appropriate shadows on the ground. Sanderson wrote:

> "These houses hung out over the road, which suddenly appeared to be muddy with large cobblestones. The houses were of (I would say) about the Elizabethan period of England, but for some reason I knew they were in Paris. They had pent roofs, with some dormer windows, gables, timbered porticoes and small windows with tiny leaded panes. Here and there, there were dull reddish lights burning behind them, as if from candles. There were iron frame lanterns hanging from timbers jutting from some houses and they were all swaying together as if in a wind, but there was not the faintest movement of the air about us."[1]

57

Sanderson must have suspected he was hallucinating, for when his wife stopped so abruptly that he walked into her he nonetheless asked her what was wrong. For a time she remained wide-eyed and speechless then ...

> "... she took my hand and, pointing, described to me exactly what I was seeing... She said, 'How did we get to Paris five hundred years ago?'" [2]

It became quite clear the Sandersons were seeing the same thing, which would seem to rule out hallucination. They compared detail after detail and pointed out various aspects of the houses to one another. Then they began to feel weak and started to sway. At that point Sanderson called to Fred, whose white shirt was still discernible in the distance.

The Sandersons felt dizzy and collapsed onto a tall, rough curbstone. Fred ran back and doled out cigarettes, by which time the strange houses and the paved road had vanished. Fred, it transpired, had seen nothing unusual.

The fact that two people mutually confirmed what they were seeing rules out any question of subjectivity. [3] The fact that Fred noticed nothing amiss indicates only that he had gone ahead of the point where the time slip occurred. If the Sandersons really had shifted to Paris, as both of them felt, their experience would conflict with the Minowski equations.

It is as well to point out, however, that the idea of Paris was no more than an impression. It was, admittedly, a shared impression, but if the houses were in the French style, it is hardly surprising that such an impression was formed. One indication that the Sandersons remained where they were in space is the fact that they never lost sight of Fred, who certainly did not go to Paris or anywhere else except up a Haitian road. Why then a time slip that produces French houses in a Caribbean island? The answer may be that Haiti was formerly a French colony. While colonization began in 1697, later than the period the Sandersons assigned to the houses, they could simply have been Haitian houses built in an earlier style.

Meanwhile, the evidence for the reality of time slips continues to mount. The author Joan Forman was in the courtyard of

Haddon Hall in Derbyshire when she noticed a group of children playing near the door. One of them was a nine-year-old girl in a lace cap and green silk dress. The group disappeared abruptly as she stepped towards them, but when she entered the Hall she discovered a portrait of the girl, the long-dead Lady Grace Manners.

This case brings up another possibility. Did Joan Forman really experience a time slip or did she see ghosts? A differential diagnosis is difficult, but the difficulty works both ways. There is a consensus opinion among psychical researchers that a great many ghostly sightings have nothing to do with spirits of the dead, but are rather something analogous to tape recordings (possibly impressed on naturally occurring electrical fields) which "play back" to certain individuals at suitable times. This consensus is based on the observation that many so-called ghosts show no awareness of the observer, but act mindlessly, as if repeating something they did centuries ago. There have even been cases of ghosts disappearing through doors which no longer exist (but once did) or walking on floors which have dropped to a different level. While the concept of a natural recording obviously fits these observations, so does time slip.

Certainly one of the most remarkable ghost stories ever, the published account of the ghosts of the Trianon Palace, has all the hallmarks of a time slip.

The story of these ghosts goes back to a hot August afternoon in 1901 when two respected and respectable Victorian ladies, on holiday in France, set out to explore the Palace of Marie Antoinette in Versailles. The first of the ladies in question was Miss Charlotte Anne Elizabeth Moberly, Principal of St. Hugh's Hall at the University of Oxford. The other was Miss Eleanor Frances Jourdain, a teacher who had founded her own girls' school in Watford. These were the days when it was thought girls needed "finishing" and the only civilized place to finish them was Paris. In order to finish her young pupils, Miss Jourdain had rented a flat in that city.

In 1901, Miss Moberly and Miss Jourdain met for the first time. Miss Moberly was impressed and suggested Miss Jourdain might like to become Vice-Principal of St. Hugh's. Before making a decision on this offer, Miss Jourdain invited Miss Moberly to stay with her in her Paris flat to see how they got on together. Miss Moberly agreed. They traveled to France for a three-week holiday and decided to visit various historic parts of Paris. One place on their itinerary was the magnificent Palace of Versailles, which is not in Paris, but is only a short distance away.

On August 10, the two traveling companions boarded a train bound for Versailles.

There is a lot to see in the former seat of the French Court. Misses Moberly and Jourdain spent much of the day touring the rooms and galleries of the palace itself, then rested in the Salle des Glaces. It was not until about four in the afternoon that Miss Moberly suggested they should visit the Petit Trianon.

The Petit Trianon is one of the minor palaces at Versailles. An imposingly columned building set in extensive and well-kept gardens, it was designed by the architect Gabriel and built during the reign of Louis XV. But the Trianon's most famous resident was undoubtedly the ill-fated Marie Antoinette, who was given the house by her husband, Louis XVI in 1774.

The Petit Trianon lies about a kilometer and a half northwest of the main palace. The two ladies consulted their guide map and set off to find it. They arrived eventually at the Grand Trianon, a companion building, and there promptly lost their way. Instead of turning right as they should have done, they went straight ahead and entered a narrow lane running roughly at right angles to the main drive. After walking north then circling a number of buildings, they asked directions from two men they took to be gardeners.

They were told to go straight on, but in their confusion managed to make a detour to the left. They passed a smallish building they described as a "kiosk" (but which they later decided must have been the Temple de l'Amour) and there, quite suddenly, began to feel distinctly strange.

"From the moment we left the lane, an extraordinary depression had come over me," Miss Moberly recorded later, "which, in spite of every effort to shake it off, steadily deepened. There seemed to be absolutely no cause for it. I was not at all tired and was becoming more interested in my surroundings."[4]

Not wanting to spoil the outing, Miss Moberly said nothing about the way she was feeling. But as it happened, Miss Jourdain was just as uncomfortable.

"There was a feeling of depression and loneliness about the place," Miss Jourdain wrote in her account of the experience. "I began to feel as if I were walking in my sleep: the heavy dreaminess was oppressive."[5]

With each determined to maintain a stiff upper lip, they continued on and, in the gardens of the Petit Trianon met (and on two occasions spoke with) a number of people, all of whom seemed to be wearing very old-fashioned clothing. The brief conversations—mainly to ask directions—were conducted in French. Both noted odd pronunciations and Miss Jourdain concluded that at least one man used an old form of the language. They emerged eventually into the front drive and the odd feeling of oppression suddenly lifted. Without discussing their experience, they took a carriage to the Hotel des Réservoirs and there had tea.

For a week, neither spoke about the Petit Trianon, but then Miss Moberly started to write a letter home and found creeping over her the same depressed mood she had felt during the Versailles visit. On impulse she asked Miss Jourdain if she thought the Petit Trianon was haunted. Miss Jourdain at once said that she did.

At this stage, the two women began to compare notes and together started to wonder about the way the people they had met were dressed. But while their suspicions were aroused, it took three months for Miss Moberly to discover that one woman she had seen was not seen at all by Miss Jourdain. Yet "it was impossible that she should not have seen the individual: for we were walking side by side and walked straight up to her, passed her and looked down upon her from the terrace."[6]

Since they now realized they had not necessarily seen the same things, they each agreed to write down a full, detailed account of what they had seen and then investigate further. Their investigations continued over a long period. It was not until three years later that they returned to Versailles and again visited the Petit Trianon.

On this visit they found it totally changed from what it had been before. It had been modernized, but by consulting the guide books and consulting officials, they soon discovered the modernization had not taken place in the last three years. There should have been no changes at all from their first visit.

Now thoroughly intrigued and perhaps a little frightened, the two ladies began to study history books which showed the Trianon as it was in the time of Louis XVI.

The features of the place then were hauntingly familiar. Their first visit, in 1901, had taken them to the Petit Trianon as it had been towards the end of the eighteenth century. They concluded that one woman they had seen might have been Marie Antoinette herself.

After publication of their account, the whole experience was rationalized away by critics who discovered a fancy dress party had been held in the Trianon by a friend of Proust called Madame de Greffuhle. It was quickly assumed the two ladies had stumbled into the celebrations and their book was allowed to go out of print in deference to the explanation, but it was an explanation soon demolished. The fancy dress party was held seven years before their Trianon visit.

The experience was not, of course, a haunting by spirits either. The entire environment was changed when the two ladies first visited it. Nor was it any sort of natural recording. The ghosts of the Trianon were aware of their modern-day visitors and quite capable of talking back. It seems that here again we are left with a time slip either of seven years (if you must cling to the fancy dress party idea) or of more than a century.

Colin Wilson reports[7] a rather more recent case which, while exhibiting several hallmarks of the traditional ghost story, is almost certainly another example of time slip. This one concerns a couple he refers to as Mr. and Mrs. Allan.

In 1954, the Allans decided on a day's break in the country and, having missed their stop on the bus, found themselves in the village of Wotton Hatch. They decided to visit the family church of the diarist John Evelyn.

As they came out of the churchyard, they decided to explore an overgrown path which led up a hill to a wooden seat with an excellent view over the valley. They were sitting on this seat eating their sandwiches when Mrs. Allan became utterly convinced three men had entered the clearing behind them. She could see them so clearly in her mind's eye that she was able to note one was wearing clerical garb. When she tried to turn around to see, she found she was paralyzed. After a few moments the feeling passed and the Allans left the clearing in a thoroughly disoriented state.

In 1956, Mrs. Allan went back. She visited the church, but could not find the path to the clearing. More to the point, the area where the path had been was flat. The hill she and her husband had climbed to get to the clearing was no longer there. She reported back to her husband, who made the same trip the following Sunday and discovered his wife was right. When he made inquiries, he found there was no wooden seat anywhere in the church grounds. The case was investigated by the Society for Psychical Research several years later. Nowhere in the area bore any resemblance to the hill, clearing and bench the Allans described, but the Society unearthed a seventeenth-century record of three criminals, one a priest, who had been executed there.

Mrs. Allan's paralysis, her mental vision of the three men, and a sudden drop in temperature noted by both she and her husband are all typical of ghostly sightings. But, no spirits of the departed, no natural tape recordings can produce a hill for you to climb and a seat for you to sit on. Only a time slip can account for that.

There was no question of ghosts in the time slip experience of Air-Marshal Sir Victor Goddard. In 1935, while still a Wing Commander, he was sent to inspect a disused airfield near Edinburgh at a place called Drem. He found it in a very dilapidated state with cattle grazing on grass that had forced through cracks in the tarmac. Later that day, he ran into trouble while flying his biplane in heavy rain and decided to fly back to Drem to get his bearings.

As he approached the airfield the torrential rain abruptly changed to bright sunlight. When he looked down he saw the airfield had been completely renovated and was now in use. There were mechanics in blue overalls walking around and four yellow planes parked on the runway. One of these was a model which, for all his aviation experience, he completely failed to recognize. It was a very puzzling experience, not alone because the instant renovation was quite impossible, but also because mechanics were supposed to wear khaki and Air Force planes were painted with a silvery aluminum paint.

Four years later, Goddard solved the mystery. With war now raging in Europe, he happened to visit Drem again ... to find it exactly as he had seen it in 1935, complete with blue-overalled mechanics and yellow planes. He even found the plane he had been unable to identify earlier—a Miles Magister.

These additional case studies support an important aspect of Minowski's calculations, but it was Arnold Toynbee who vindicated the whole of the Minowski picture. You will recall that the equations show the whole of an individual's past and future always meet at a single point defined by the position of the observer at a specific location in space-time. Toynbee's specific location in space-time was the southern section of the Buckingham Palace Road in London just after the start of the First World War when he "... found himself in communion not just with this or that episode in History, but with all that has been and was and was to come."[8]

Toynbee described how he became "directly aware" of the passage of history gently flowing through him in a mighty current, with his own life welling like a wave in the flow of this vast tide. What he saw as history might more properly be described as time. Toynbee had somehow become personally aware of the precise structure described in the Minowski equations.

Endnotes

1. Sanderson, Ivan. *Things and More Things*, Pyramid Books, New York, 1967.

2. Quoted by Colin Wilson in *Beyond the Occult*, Corgi, London, 1989.

3. Since it has become fashionable to evoke mutual telepathic hallucination as an explanation in cases of this sort, I suppose I should make two points. The first is that there is nothing in the annals of psychical research to suggest mutual telepathic hallucination is remotely possible. The second is that this explanation is selectively applied to situations we

find difficult to believe. If mutual telepathic hallucinations are a fact of life, they are just as likely to arise in a report by my wife and I that we visited a restaurant last night.

4. Quoted by Colin Wilson in *Beyond the Occult*, Corgi, London, 1989.

5. Ibid.

6. Ibid.

7. Ibid.

8. *A Study of History vol. 10*, Oxford University Press, 1954.

CHAPTER TEN

With the possible exception of the Sandersons' experience in Haiti, every quoted case study aligns itself with an aspect of the Minowski equations, but only one of them—Sir Victor Goddard's flight over Drem—is supported by Einstein's Special Theory of Relativity as a whole. Einstein showed, with his famous twins paradox that time travel of a sort was possible ... but only one way. Relative astronauts might shift in time in relation to their relative relatives, but only from the present into the future. When we search for travel through time in the Special Theory of Relativity, what we find is really more akin to acceleration through time. The astronaut twin zips along the timestream so quickly he gets to a distant future far sooner than his twin on Earth.[1]

What makes the Special Theory of Relativity special is that it doesn't work very well. Or, more accurately, that it only works in a limited set of circumstances. It does not, for example, work at all if there is gravity about.

Gravity has always been a bother to physicists. Newton described its laws, but not how the Earth managed to reach up to grab the apple. This is action at a distance, and it was dismissed as an occult fancy by several of his detractors. One of them, Leibniz, sneeringly suggested it must be "the effect of a miracle." They were, of course, quite right and generations of physicists were to battle with the problems posed by gravity without ever explaining how action at a distance actually came about.

In 1916, Einstein pulled off another of his spectacular tricks. In much the same way he had swallowed whole the paradox of the speed of light, he went on to swallow whole the problem of gravity.

It is probably true to say that until 1916, scientists, like the rest of us, believed gravity was some sort of force, like kinetic energy or magnetism. Einstein, after long hard thought, decided that it wasn't. The process started in 1907, when he announced his principle of equivalence.

I got to understand the principle of equivalence the day I bought a sports car. The difference between it and my previous banger was that it was turbo charged and had a higher power-to-weight ratio. As a result, every time I put my foot down, the seat slammed into my back. This exciting phenomenon was the result of acceleration.

Acceleration influences your weight. If you stand on a pair of bathroom scales in a rocket, you can watch your weight double, triple, and keep on climbing until you reach escape velocity when mission control cuts the thrust and suddenly your weight drops to nothing as you float in free-fall beyond the Earth's atmosphere.

Science fiction writers and science writers (who are often the same people) have also noticed what happens when you put your foot down in a turbo and stand on bathroom scales in a rocket. They long ago suggested that if we ever get around to building seriously large space stations—the sort that will hold whole colonies of people for months or years at a time—we should set them spinning in order to generate artificial gravity. In 1907, Einstein said there was nothing artificial about it. Gravity and acceleration were equivalent. This isn't quite saying they're both the same thing. What he actually said was that in a closed system there's absolutely no way of distinguishing between the two, which is very close indeed to saying they're both the same thing.

Einstein wasn't satisfied. In hot pursuit of a theory of physics, which would explain just about everything there was to explain, he traveled to Zürich, Switzerland, to look up an old school friend, Marcel Grossman, by now a professor of geometry. "Marcel," he said, "you must help me otherwise I'll go crazy." And Grossman, when he heard the problem, said, "You need to look at Riemann."[2]

In order to understand this snatch of conversation, you need to know that what you were taught about geometry in high school was a little bit off the wall. That geometry was based on the work of Euclid.

For a Greek more famous than Zorba, surprisingly little is known about Euclid. He lived between 320 and 260 B.C. and taught at Alexandria in Egypt and that's about as much as we can find out. But Euclid's *Elements*, an introductory work on geometry, became the most influential mathematical textbook in history. It begins with definitions, postulates, and axioms, including the famous parallel postulate you learned at school. That's the one which states only one line can be drawn parallel to a given line through a given point.

Euclid put this forward as a self-evident assumption and built his whole mighty edifice of geometry upon it. Over a thousand editions of his book have been published since the first printed version of 1482, each generating a multitude of commentaries, precis, and restatements of his findings. Multitudes of children have learned that the three angles of a triangle always add up to 180 degrees, that the square on the hypotenuse is equal to the sum of the squares on the other two sides, that the circumference of a circle is $2\pi R$ and a host of other useful conclusions, all based on that self-evident assumption about the parallel lines and the given point.

In the nineteenth century a few lunatic mathematicians began to wonder what would happen if the parallel postulate, against all common sense and experience, simply wasn't true. They held onto Euclid's first four postulates, but modified the fifth. The result was the development of two new geometries—hyperbolic and elliptic.

Hyperbolic geometry is based on the assumption that there are at least two lines passing through a given point that are parallel to a given line. Elliptic geometry, by contrast, starts with the idea that there aren't any. When you think about it, these three cases—one line (Euclid), two or more lines (hyperbolic), and no lines at all (elliptic)—cover every possibility.

Both hyperbolic and elliptic geometries are internally consistent. That's to say, once you change the initial Euclidean postulate and work from there, everything hangs together just as logically as it did with the stuff you learned at school. But the conclusions are quite different. In hyperbolic geometry, for example, the angles of a triangle always add up to less than 180 degrees and its area is proportional to the difference between the sum of its angles and 180 degrees. Just the opposite occurs in elliptic geometry, and neither of the two agree with Euclid. You can't even get similar triangles with different areas in either of the two non-Euclidean geometries.

The people mainly responsible for this mess were the Hungarian Janos Bolyai and the Russian Nicolai Lobachevsky, who developed the principles of hyperbolic geometry between them in the nineteenth century. The Riemann mentioned to Einstein by Marcel Grossman was Georg Friedrich Bernhard Riemann, one of the most influential nineteenth-century German mathematicians. He developed elliptic geometry in his paper *Uber die Hypothesen, welche der Geometrie zu Grunde liegen* (*On the Hypotheses Which Lie at the Foundation of Geometry*), published in 1854.

It is probably true to say that, for most people, non-Euclidean geometries were intricate works of fiction, curiosities disconnected from the real world. The recognition of their validity was resisted by many who proclaimed with religious fervor that Euclidean geometry had an exclusive handle on the truth. But this reflects a failure to recognize that a geometry is a mathematical system determined by its assumptions. How far any geometry (including Euclid's) represents the real world has to be a matter of observation.

Two thousand years or more of observation has shown Euclidean geometry works very well in this neck of the woods. You would be hard put to find me a triangle whose angles did not add up to 180 degrees. Nonetheless, such triangles can be found and not just in the theoretical notepads of Georg Riemann.

What was frustrating Einstein when he made his plea to Grossman was that he had a mental picture of space-time that just wouldn't work for him. It explained a lot, but it didn't explain gravity. In pointing him towards Riemann, Grossman was suggesting what he needed was a space-time that obeyed the rules of elliptic geometry instead of Euclidean. Einstein very quickly found he was right.

If you stand on Salisbury Plain in England, staring gloomily at what the authorities have done to Stonehenge, the world looks flat. It's only when you take the shuttle that it starts to look the way it really is—a sphere. Space itself, Einstein discovered, is a bit like that. When you draw your triangles and make your measurements on a human scale, Euclidean geometry works perfectly, because on this scale space is as near flat as makes no difference. When you start to consider space in the macrocosm—the space of galaxies, measured in par secs and light years—the curve begins to show.

I'm speaking figuratively, you understand. You can't actually see the curve of space however far out in the universe you stand because you're still standing in space, still seeing things from the local perspective. But if you can't see curved space, you can certainly infer it from other observations. This is what Einstein had been trying to do. Now, thanks to the timely word from Grossman, he realized space was curved and that it obeyed the laws of Riemannian geometry.

Exactly a month before Christmas in 1915, Einstein presented his new paper, The Field Equations of Gravitation, to the Prussian Academy of Sciences. What the scientists on the evaluation committee read was, at long last, the General Theory of Relativity.

All of which brings us full circle to the problem of gravity. Having nudged it to the edge in 1907 by saying it was equivalent to acceleration, he now pushed it all the way over in 1915 by suggesting it didn't actually exist at all—not as a force at any rate. Gravity, he figured, was just an illusion created by the way objects moved in space-time.

It took the visual mind of Bertrand Russell to make sense of that for the rest of us. Russell suggested you imagine you were born in a balloon hovering at night above a lighted beacon on the ground below. There are people down there. You can see their torches flickering as they walk about.

Watching those torches, you notice something peculiar. The torches usually move in a straight line, but when they happen to approach the beacon, that changes. Some of them curve around the beacon in a wide arc. Others approach it closer in a straight line, but then deflect away from it. After a while you have worked out one of the basic laws of the beacon: the closer you get to it, the more sharply you're deflected. Since you have nothing else to do in the balloon, you try to figure out what's going on.

You probably conclude very quickly there is something about that beacon that repels anybody approaching it. Maybe it was too hot to get really close. Maybe it was giving off a dangerous radiation. Maybe it was releasing quantities of deadly gas. Maybe it was an enormous electromagnet and the people below were wearing metallic suits of the same polarization.

If you were still trying to figure it out when dawn breaks, you would find, according to Russell, that none of these very obvious ideas was even remotely close to the truth. The reality of the situation was that the beacon was situated on top of a mountain, which grew progressively steep towards its summit. The only reason the people with the torches didn't come near the beacon was that they were following the various paths around the mountain. The higher the path they chose, the nearer they came to the beacon and the more sharply they veered away because of the steeper incline of the terrain. What you were really looking at was people taking the easiest way to get to where they wanted to go—it just looked different in the dark.

Einstein started to think space-time might look different in the daytime. He pictured it as a terrain and calculated that it was distorted by the presence of large masses of matter, like a planet or, even more spectacularly, a sun. Our sun was the mountain of the beacon analogy. The orbits of the planets could be explained as the easiest space-time routes around the mountain. Don't imagine his 1915 paper put it like that. The Field Equations of Gravitation was exactly what its name implies—a series of formulae, which expressed specific structures. If you feed observed information into those formulae you get an idea of what space and time must be like. What comes out the other end is the picture of space-time distorted by mass to give a pseudo-terrain peppered by hills and mountains.

Einstein suspected it went even further than that. He suspected it wasn't really a question of matter distorting space-time. He suspected that matter actually was the distortion in space-time. This is a vision reminiscent of mystical consciousness. It suggests there's no such thing as gravity, no such thing as matter, no such thing as energy. There's only space-time. What we see as a planet circling a sun, its orbit held in place by the force of gravity, is really a bump in space-time finding its way around a bigger bump by the easiest route. It's a mind-blowing prospect and, unfortunately, Einstein, who died in 1955, was never able to prove it.

What he did prove in the realm of General Relativity had a lot of relevance to our prospects for time travel.

Endnotes

1. Who, in any case, only survives long enough to make part of the trip.
2. Coveny and Highfield, *The Arrow of Time*. Flamingo, London. 1991

CHAPTER ELEVEN

If gravity is equivalent to acceleration, and acceleration, as we noted in the Twins Paradox, can influence the flow of time, then you might be forgiven for wondering whether gravity can influence the flow of time as well. Einstein reckoned that it could. He calculated that where there was gravity, clocks ticked more slowly. Where there was a lot of gravity, clocks ticked very slowly indeed. He called the effect gravitational time dilation.

In 1924, Einstein visited the California Institute of Technology in Pasadena and was entertained to a dinner in his honor. A high point of the evening came when Professor W. H. Williams read a poem he had composed for the occasion titled *The Einstein and the Eddington*. The Eddington in question was Arthur Eddington, who had already confirmed an important aspect of General Relativity. Williams' poem, a parody on Lewis Carroll, went in part:

'The time has come,' said Eddington,
'To talk of many things.
Of cubes and clocks and meter-sticks,
And why a pendulum swings,
And how far space is out of plumb,
And whether time has wings.
You hold that time is badly warped,
That even light is bent
I think I get the idea there,
If this is what you meant
The mail the postman brings today,
Tomorrow will be sent.'
'The shortest line,' Einstein replied,
'Is not the one that's straight
It curves around upon itself,
Much like a figure eight,
And if you go too rapidly,

You will arrive too late.
But Easter Day is Christmas time,
And far away is near,
And two and two is more than four
And over there is here.'
'You may be right,' said Eddington.
'It seems a trifle queer.'[1]

General Relativity was altogether too queer to be accepted without some very solid proof, but proof was not long coming. The first indication that Einstein might be right arose in the world of astronomy. For years, an anomaly in the orbit of Mercury had more or less convinced astronomers there was another planet hidden in the solar system. An extra gravitational field was the only thing that could explain the peculiar way Mercury moved. The problem was they couldn't find the missing planet.

This in itself was odd. Modern telescopes are excellent, the solar system is relatively small, a planet generating enough gravity to influence Mercury had to be a substantial object, and it would have to be orbiting in the well-charted inner reaches of the system. There was some discussion about the possibility that this extra planet, already named Vulcan, always remained hidden from Earth by the sun itself, but that would require an orbit exactly synchronized with our own—not quite an impossibility, but a coincidence so extreme most scientists found it difficult to swallow.

With the publication of Einstein's theory in 1916, the problem was suddenly solved. If you stopped examining Mercury using Newtonian physics and applied Einstein's new General Theory of Relativity, the peculiar motion of Mercury was explained perfectly—without the need of any hidden planet. Mercury was the most troublesome case, but smaller anomalies in the orbits of other planets have since been shown to be General Relativity effects.

Einstein's prediction that light would be bent by a gravitational field was confirmed by Eddington in 1919. That was the year when a solar eclipse made it possible to measure the starlight usually hidden by the sun's glare. Eddington, who like Professor Williams had a poetic turn of mind, returned from his eclipse observations in the Gulf of Guinea to announce at a Royal Astronomical Society dinner:

> Oh leave the Wise our Measures to collate.
> One thing at least is certain, light has weight
> One thing is certain and the rest debate—
> Light rays, when near the Sun, do not go straight![2]

Bent light and planetary anomalies were one thing, but time distortion quite another. All the same, Einstein's prediction that time is bent by gravity was to hold up just as well as his prediction about gravity bending light.

A few years ago, increasing public awareness of ecology led, among other things, to vastly increased sales of little electronic gadgets called ionizers. These are machines that generate negative ions, and when there are lots of negative ions about, human beings feel good. In nature, negative ions are created by moving water, which explains why it's nice to have a picnic beside a waterfall. They are also generated when you stroke a cat, but the greatest source of ions, negative and positive, is the sun, a fact that allowed the first verification of Einstein's ideas about gravity and time.

Ions are electrically charged atoms. The sun manufactures them by the billion and sends them streaming into space. As they move, they oscillate. It is a very precise oscillation determined by the exact and unvarying frequencies of the electrons circling the atomic nucleus. In other words, an ion is an almost unimaginably accurate clock.

Once you realize that, you realize you have a way to test General Relativity predictions about time. If Einstein was right, then ions in the massive gravitational field of the sun should oscillate more slowly than ions on Earth where gravity is a lot weaker. You can tell how fast an ion is oscillating by the wavelength of its radiation, which lengthens as the oscillation slows.

When measurements were made of ion wavelengths in the sun's gravitational field, astrophysicists discovered Einstein was right: they were slightly longer than they should be. Since there wasn't much in it, they then went on to measure ion radiation from white dwarfs, a type of star which has substantially more of a gravitational field. Sure enough, the wavelength was significantly longer. Crazy though it seemed, time ran slower on heavy-gravity bodies.

During the winter of 1975, Carroll Alley, a scientist at the University of Maryland, actually managed to show there are differences in the rate of time-flow on Earth depending on local gravitational conditions. Alley used two groups of super-accurate atomic clocks, one of which stayed on the ground while the other was flown around Chesapeake Bay at a height of 20,000 feet. Even when he adjusted for the effect of motion (which we already know influences time) he still found a differential between the clocks on the ground and the clocks on the plane. It was tiny— measured literally in billionths of a second—but it was there, and it was caused by the fact that the further you move away from the center of the Earth, the weaker gravity becomes.

With the gravitational influence on time now firmly established, it is possible to postulate a second time machine similar to our near-light-speed rocket. All you need do is subject one of the twins to a far greater gravity field than the other and the high gravity twin will age more slowly, effectively traveling into his sibling's future. Unfortunately, you're likely to squash the high-gravity twin flat before you get a really useful time dilation effect—he would be crushed by his own weight while standing on a white dwarf. All the same, the theory remains valid, even if the practical difficulties still cause problems to our current technology.

It is, however, important to note one fact: even in theory, you can only send the high gravity twin one way. Exactly like his near-light-speed counterpart, he hurtles towards the future, never towards the past.

Endnotes:

1. Quoted by Coveny and Highfield in *The Arrow of Time*.
2. Ibid.

CHAPTER TWELVE

Einstein's General Theory of Relativity presented a whole new way of looking at the universe, one in which energy, time, space, and matter were intimately connected. He confirmed the insights of Special Relativity, which showed it was a fundamental error to consider space and time as two distinct things. He replaced them with the single concept of space-time, a continuum which embraced both.

Against the background of this insight, Einstein went on to show that matter distorted the space-time continuum, an effect we experience as gravity. Thus, gravity is not a force in the traditional sense, but a wrinkle or twist in the fabric of space-time. If you collect together enough matter in one place, the distortion of space-time becomes so pronounced that the fabric actually rips. What results is a Black Hole.

A Black Hole is the remains of a star whose surface gravity is so strong nothing can escape from it. The root concept far predates Einstein. In 1798, the French mathematician Pierre Simon de Laplace published a treatise in which he reasoned that if enough mass were added to a star like the Sun, its gravitational force would become so great that its escape velocity would equal the speed of light. At that point, light would not be able to leave the surface of the star. It would blink out and become invisible.

Einstein's insight that nothing can move faster than light meant Laplace's black stars had to be Black Holes, because if light can't get out, nothing else can either. The actual term "Black Hole" was coined in 1967 by the American physicist John Wheeler while speaking at a conference in New York, but the theory had emerged nine years earlier. Another American physicist, David Finkelstein of Yeshiva University in New York, calculated that General Relativity must, under certain circumstances, produce what he called a one-way membrane. One-way membranes, Finkelstein claimed, came into being under extreme gravity. They were essentially a threshold over which physical objects and even light would pass never to return. The surface of a Black Hole acts like a Finkelstein membrane: material may fall into a Black Hole, but no information or energy can come out.

Finkelstein talked about his theory at the University of London the following year. It excited a graduate student named Roger Penrose (now among the big names of international physics) so much that he developed it into the modern theory of the Black Hole. Outside of scientific note pads, Black Holes are associated with stars too large to sustain their own weight—which effectively means any star more than three times larger than our sun. At a particular stage of its evolution, such a star begins to collapse in on itself, becoming smaller and smaller, more and more dense. The first stage of this collapse is the formation of a neutron star.

Neutron stars are extremely small, high-density stellar corpses composed of tightly packed subatomic particles. Their existence was first put forward in 1932 by the Soviet physicist Lev Landau who theorized about a state of matter that was stable only at massively high densities. Just how dense is indicated by the fact scientists now estimate that in a neutron star, a mass the size of our sun is packed into a sphere only twelve and a half miles in diameter.

Neutron stars remained a theory until 1967 when British radio astronomers Jocelyn Bell Burnell and Antony Hewish finally found one. It was the weirdest thing they'd ever come across, a stellar body that emitted regular pulses of electromagnetic radiation, mainly radio waves. The following year the idea was put forward that pulsars were actually rotating neutron stars—the short period and the regularity of the pulses suggested a small, massive star of the kind predicted by theory. A consensus soon formed that this suggestion was correct.

Many neutron stars stay neutron stars, spinning wildly and exciting radio astronomers with their pulses. But as long ago as 1917 a German astrophysicist named Karl Schwarzschild used Einstein's new General Theory of Relativity to calculate that if the star you started with was big enough, once it collapsed beyond a critical radius, it would become a Black Hole. The critical radius is now known as the Schwarzschild radius in his honor.

The hypothetical sphere marked by the Schwarzschild radius is called the event horizon, the point at which escape velocity just equals the speed of light. If a star the size of our Sun could become a Black Hole—which it won't in reality because it doesn't have enough mass—this radius would be about three kilometers, or two miles. To find the Schwarzschild radius of any other object, double its mass multiplied by the universal gravitational constant and divide your result by the speed of light.

In the vicinity of a Black Hole, many of the laws of physics—and all the laws of common sense—break down. Mathematicians calculate that at the heart of a Black Hole there must exist what is called a singularity, an area where certain values reach infinity. We have already noted that scientists are suspicious of singularities and when you discover what a singularity can do in a Black Hole you soon see why.

If you have the misfortune to fall into a static Black Hole, by the time you reach the singularity, your volume will have been reduced to zero (an impossibility, but never mind) and you will be in an environment where space and time have literally ceased to exist. The calculations surrounding the singularity of a static Black Hole so brutalize the familiar laws of physics that scientists have begun to speculate on the possibility that you would not really be reduced to zero volume at all, but rather sucked through the fabric of space-time into a wholly different universe. They don't, however, like to speculate on what state you would be in when you got there.

Scientists don't like the idea of an alternative universe. Einstein himself saw that General Theory might point towards one and tended towards the belief that there was a flaw in his theory. All the same, he had the intellectual courage to publish his findings in 1935. The paper was co-authored by his colleague Nathan Rosen. It represented a wholly unexpected development. A Black Hole, at that point, was thought of as an area of such intense gravity that it sucked everything into itself from its immediate vicinity. Nothing whatsoever could escape. But the calculations of Einstein and Rosen showed that an essential aspect of this ultimate vacuum cleaner was that it had to be paired with a White

Hole, an area of space in which matter and light were spewed out at the same rate as matter and light entered the Black Hole.

The problem was the corresponding White Hole could not exist in this universe. It was, so to speak, the other side of the Black Hole and had to be elsewhere—in another, separate continuum of reality. The crossover point between the Black Hole on this side and the White Hole on the other side became known as an Einstein-Rosen bridge.

If Einstein found that discovery unpalatable, worse was to come. The concept of two (and only two) parallel universes arises out of calculations based on a static Black Hole. In the real world, Black Holes are unlikely to be static. It is a fact of astronomical observation that virtually all celestial bodies are in motion. The Earth spins on its own axis, so does the Sun, so do most stars. If our collapsing neutron star is spinning, it will carry this characteristic into the Black Hole phase. The result is a spinning Black Hole.

In 1963, the Australian physicist Roy P. Kerr showed that a spinning Black Hole is the focal point of an infinite number of parallel universes, all but one of which are theoretically accessible from this one.

If a static Black Hole is very bad news for a careless astronaut, the calculations indicate a spinning Black Hole might be sort of interesting. The singularity of a spinning Black Hole is shaped like a ring, not a solid sphere. So, if you got lucky when you fell in, you might miss it altogether. If you did, physicists believe there is a possibility that you might get through the Black Hole—not necessarily in one piece—to emerge in a different area of space. Is there also a possibility that you might emerge in a different time?

CHAPTER THIRTEEN

Science writer Gary Zukav called Black Holes "the ultimate time machines."[1] But could they ever be used as such? In 1917, when Schwarzschild made his calculations and even in 1935 when Einstein and Rosen published their joint paper, nobody was even sure Black Holes existed outside the continuum of pure mathematics. In other words they were, at that time, theoretical constructions which might or might not have had any counterpart in the real world. Things have changed since then.

The first thing that has changed is physicists no longer believe a Black Hole is black. Although, by definition, light from our own space-time continuum is sucked in and can't escape, photons and other particles from the universes beyond may well get through the one-way membrane via a process known as quantum tunneling. We'll be looking at quantum physics a little later. For now, it's enough to say some scientists believe Black Holes may shine.

Even if Black Holes remain genuinely invisible, they still send out massive signals of their presence. One signal is X-rays. This comes about because the Black Hole sucks in hydrogen and various other atoms and particles. As they approach the Black Hole, they accelerate. If you accelerate any charged particle, it gives off radiation. With the Black Hole accelerating just about every particle in sight, there has to be a lot of radiation about. If you're looking for a Black Hole, look for a (probably) dark area of space that is radiating X-rays wildly.

Another signal is gravity. As we have already noted, Black Holes are the greatest gravity generators in the universe. If there happens to be a normal visible star in the neighborhood, it will be influenced by the gravitational field. It may be drawn into orbit around the Black Hole. Stellar matter may be sucked from it into the Black Hole. In some cases, the star may eventually be swallowed whole. So, if you find a star behaving oddly, particularly if it seems to be orbiting an invisible body, then there is a good chance it may be a binary system partnered with a Black Hole.

(There is also the possibility of a sort of early warning system indicating that a Black Hole is about to form. If the collapsing star is not spherical, perhaps because it was flattened at the poles, General Relativity predicts gravitational waves will be given off just before the critical transformation. Gravitational waves are theoretical disturbances of the gravitational field. They travel at the speed of light and affect the motion of other objects—they are, in short, analogous to electromagnetic waves. Their existence has not yet been confirmed, but detectors are currently being built.)

In 1970, an orbiting astronomical satellite picked up one of these signals in the constellation Cygnus, located in the Northern Hemisphere some eleven light years from our Earth. Something in Cygnus was generating a million times more electromagnetic radiation than our sun. Astronomers, who named the source Cygnus X-1, then noticed a blue supergiant seemed to be orbiting around it. With both signs in place, the conclusion was the first Black Hole had actually been found. Five years later, the British satellite Ariel identified another X-ray source. Soon afterwards, a third was found in the Large Megellanic Cloud. Since then, more than a hundred similar sets of signals have been picked up.

Black holes may come in an extreme range of sizes. The English physicist Stephen Hawking has speculated that tiny Black Holes, the size of elementary particles, may have been formed by the big bang that gave birth to the universe. At the other extreme, gigantic Black Holes may exist, as massive as a hundred million Suns, at the center of galaxies. A possible massive Black Hole has been reported in the center of M 87, a giant elliptical radio galaxy. So, Black Holes aren't exactly commonplace, but there are still quite a few of them about.

The question is, could a man from our distant future have sailed his spaceship through a Black Hole then returned to Earth 500 million years ago to leave his footprint in the Utah mud? There are obviously immense technical problems to such a scenario, but is it at least theoretically possible?

The Princeton physicist Martin Kruskal was one of the first to attempt an accurate map of the inside of a Black Hole. He started with the singularity represented by the Schwarzschild radius.

A singularity is a mathematical construction in which certain values reach infinity. When scientists reach a singularity, they usually take it to mean their theory has just broken down. They do not normally assume that such a singularity exists in the real world. There are many physicists who believe this is exactly the case with Black Holes. Einstein's General Theory of Relativity predicted their existence. Astronomers are now virtually certain they have been found. But when you come to the crunch, General Relativity is useless in describing what actually happens inside a Black Hole. If you apply the theory, you get a singularity and a singularity means the theory is fraying at the edges.

This is a very reasonable stance. Nobody has ever detected a singularity in the real world. This does not mean a singularity couldn't exist in a Black Hole—after all, conditions in there are pretty extreme—but it does mean you shouldn't bank on it.

The last time scientists came up with what looked like a real singularity was in the world of cartography. In map-making, as you probably know, our globe is divided up into lines of latitude and longitude. If you want to draw a triangle on the globe, you must have one leg parallel to a line of longitude and one leg parallel to a line of latitude. This works beautifully so long as you don't try to draw a triangle which has one of its corners at the North Pole.[2] Lines of latitude vanish at the poles so if you try to draw your triangle, you get a singularity.

Except that you don't really. You can still draw your triangle using a different coordinate map—one using lines that cross at right angles on a plane, for example. Your singularity wasn't a real singularity—that's to say it didn't exist in the real world. It only arose because you were looking at things the wrong way. You were using the wrong map.

Kruskal started to wonder if maybe we weren't looking at Black Holes the wrong way. He started to tinker around with a new map. To get rid of the singularity he had to find a new set of coordinates perpendicular to each other, but that weren't the normal space/time coordinates we all use for measurement.

If this sounds as if he was diving down a rabbit hole, you are forgetting relativity. As Einstein showed, viewpoint is everything.

The acid test of reality is no longer common sense, but whether or not you can find a viewpoint in the physical universe from which your ideas are possible. Incredibly, Kruskal found such a viewpoint. If you are a zero-time particle whizzing towards a Black Hole, the singularity marked by the Schwarzschild radius no longer exists. Your new viewpoint has given you the missing co-ordinates. Do zero-time particles occur in the real world? The answer is a definite yes. You are surrounded by billions of them as you read these words. Zero-time particles are photons, the essential components of light.

The new viewpoint didn't get rid of the other singularity in the Black Hole—the one at the center where gravity becomes infinite—but it did split it in two and place the halves in a different position. This still suggested General Relativity had broken down as a theory, but it also suggested the Black Hole had symmetry. Physicists love symmetry almost as much as they hate singularities and for much the same reason. If singularities suggest your theory is breaking down, symmetry suggests you may be on the right track. So, Kruskal decided to live with his two new singularities for the sake of his symmetry. He went ahead and made his map.

Kruskal's map of the inside of a Black Hole is exciting. It showed four separate zones. Two of these zones contained the new singularities. The other two were our universe and a parallel, different, brand new, hitherto unsuspected space-time continuum. In short, another universe. In that other universe, time flows backwards.

Physicist Fred A. Wolf described what would happen to an astronaut passing through the sort of Black Hole Kruskal mapped:

> "As soon as he crosses the critical radius, he will begin to see a point of light at the center of the hole. Darkness will surround the point of light and a halo of light from his universe will surround the dark... As he gets closer to the singularity at the center, the point of light will bloom out into a sphere of light ...
>
> Just as he crosses the critical Schwartzchild surface, he will see infinity. All of the universe's history to be will pass

before him in a flash—for the universe he left will have aged remarkably quickly.

He will then cross over into the Black Hole and begin to see the other universe. However, he will still see a light halo coming from his universe. This halo will appear to him as the same movie he just watched, only this time running backwards in time. Thus he will see all the events of his past coming to him in a time-reversed sense ...."[3]

Time travel? Not quite, for Wolf's hypothetical astronaut is wholly out of control. He might like to stop at a particular point in the time reversal, but he can't. He is being sucked, along with space and time itself, through the tube-like structure of the Black Hole. In moments (if that phrase has any meaning in the circumstances), he will be hurled into the parallel universe. And while time may flow backwards there, this does him no good at all. He cannot access the past or future he wishes to access, because they no longer exist, other than in the universe he left.

Of course, both Kruskal's map and Wolf's description were based on a static Black Hole. How do things look in a spinning Black Hole?

The first thing to note is that it has two event horizons, one inside the other. The first of these is identical to the event horizon of a static Black Hole, but the second is its absolute reverse. Passing through the first switches space and time: you are no longer able to move in space except in the direction of the pull, but you are now able to move any way you want in time. Passing through the second switches things back again: time and space start to behave the way they always did. Hitting the singularity in the middle brings you in contact with an area of negative space where the reversal of gravity will spit you out like an apple pip. Fortunately, when we turn to the calculations of Roy Kerr, the physicist who mapped spinning Black Holes, there is nothing to insist you will hit the singularity. If you avoid it, you can take your pick of exits—all of them leading into parallel universes, and none of them requiring you to travel faster than the speed of light, hence theoretically accessible. Fred Wolf again:

"First, he would cross the outer event horizon and enter the inner space of the hole—the region where his normal space and time orientation become reversed. In this region he will be compelled to move on, never returning to our universe again...

Next, he will pass through the inner event horizon and enter the zone just adjacent to the singularity. As long as the hole keeps on spinning he will pass right on by the singularity. It is no longer a "spacelike" singularity compelling him to fall into it. Since time and space have reversed once again, time is back on track. The singularity no longer holds any fear for him...

Soon, he will pass out of the innermost region, passing once again through an inner event horizon. Again time and space will reverse for him and he will be compelled to move on out. When he crosses the outer event horizon, he will then pass into a parallel universe—a whole new world...

If his trajectory is true enough he will pass into his parallel past, possibly reaching the time of his birth. If the second universe is an exact copy of his universe, he will see himself being born again.[4]

Fred Wolf theorized that the concept of parallel worlds was the key to time travel:

"Gone-by and yet-to-be are simply reference points based on our sense of now. They are simultaneous with us in the parallel worlds view of time.

These pasts and futures are ... side-by-side parallel universes. The past and future which we remember are just those time wave clashes with greatest strengths and most resonance." [5]

He visualized the past and future worlds not exactly as our own past and future, but rather mirror images of our past and future stretching to infinity. If we could enter one of these reflections, like Alice climbing through the looking-glass, we could, for all practical purposes, travel in time. If there were subtle differences in the next continuum, it is unlikely we would even notice them. After all, how aware are you of the fact that when you stand before a mirror and raise your right arm, it's the left arm that's raised by your reflection?

If you want to enter the reflected past or future of your world, however, would it be literally possible to take the Black Hole trip described by Dr. Wolf and survive? Physicists by and large say no. Long before you could get close enough to a Black Hole to benefit from its peculiarities, gravity would have become so strong that the differential between your head and your feet would be enough to rip you apart.

We need to be careful here. The whole history of science is littered with impossibilities—Iron ships won't float—You'll never get it off the ground—which subsequently proved to be no more than technical problems. There was a time when physicists believed the human body could not withstand the stresses of speeds that exceeded a galloping horse. What the physicists describe as the prime danger of a Black Hole is a technical problem, not a theoretical impossibility. Anyone who states categorically that technology can never get around it has forgotten the red faces of those who predicted confidently rockets would never work in space because their exhaust gases had nothing to push against.

All the same, is it worth risking life and limb in a Black Hole? It may offer time travel, but only of a sort. You are not permitted to reach the past, merely a copy of the past. It may look the same and feel the same and smell the same and taste the same, but it's still a copy and, human nature being what it is, the reproduction Van Gogh is nowhere near so valuable as the real thing. Besides, it seems touch and go whether even a Black Hole will permit you to travel beyond the confines of your (copied?) personal timeline. Interesting though the investigation has been, we may have to look further for the origins of the Utah footprint.

Endnotes

1. In his immensely readable overview of the new physics, *The Dancing Wu Li Masters*, Fontana Books, London, 1982.

2. Or South Pole for that matter.

3. Wolf, Fred Alan. *Parallel Universes*. Touchstone Books, New York, 1990.

4. Ibid.

5. Ibid.

CHAPTER FOURTEEN

In the early 1960s, the distinguished science fiction author Ray Bradbury published a story in *Playboy* magazine called *The Sound of Thunder*. It described the operations of Time Safaris, Inc., a company that specialized in taking clients back in time to hunt animals now extinct.

In the story, a group returned to Jurassic times to hunt the most dangerous prey of them all—Tyrannosaurus Rex, the largest of the meat-eating dinosaurs. Time Safari executives were very sensitive to the possibility of influencing the future by their activities in the past so prey animals were hunted only if they were about to die anyway and all time travelers were rigorously confined to a levitating metal path to ensure they did not inadvertently damage the local flora.

The hunted tyrannosaur was scheduled to die less than an hour after the time travelers arrived, crushed by a falling tree. Members of the safari were sternly warned about the dangers of interacting with the past in any way that might potentially influence the future, but when the tyrannosaur appeared, one of them was so overwhelmed that he left the path and stepped on a butterfly. It was a small thing, but when the group returned to their own time, they discovered their benevolent political regime had been replaced by a neo-Fascist dictatorship.

Bradbury's story stresses an important point. If time travel into the past ever does become possible, our descendants will have to take great care to avoid any action which would influence the future. It may be that the nature of time or time travel will automatically preclude outright paradoxes. Even without them, Bradbury showed that the smallest influence could potentially have very unpleasant results.

If this idea is correct, it allows us to speculate on the regulations likely to govern time travel in the future. Should you insist on traveling to an historical past, you would have to take great care to blend in with the contemporary culture, to avoid interfering in politics or customs (however repulsive they might be) and to ensure you did not introduce paradoxical technology. Bradbury's story notwithstanding, it would probably be deemed safer to travel to a distant past. Strolling through Gondwanaland[1] at a time before our familiar life forms had evolved would probably be less risky than a trip of just a century or so... even if you were careless enough to lose a cargo of metal spheres in what would one day become South Africa.

These regulations, like all regulations, would have to be balanced against human nature, something which has changed only marginally in the last ten thousand years and is likely to change only marginally in the next. Human nature would drive our descendants to explore the more interesting areas of time whatever the risk. One such area, as Bradbury ably predicted, is the Triassic, Jurassic and Cretaceous periods, the great Mesozoic Era of the dinosaurs.

As Michael Crichton and Steven Spielberg established in their vastly successful *Jurassic Park*, dinosaurs are likely to be the greatest tourist attraction of all time. However many restrictions are laid down by the real Time Safari companies of tomorrow, the sheer volume of tourists will ensure mistakes must be made. These may not lead to the establishment of Fascist dictatorships,[2] but they should leave traces. Not many, perhaps, since we are speaking of a period which stretches from 65 million to 213 million years before our own time, but there should, perhaps, be something.

Interestingly enough, there is.

In 1968, archaeologists investigating fossil remnants in a chalk bed exposed by quarrying operations at Saint-Jean de Livet in France, came upon a number of semi-ovoid metallic tubes. They varied in size, but were identical in shape. Unlike the metal spheres found in South Africa, there could be no question of their being concretions. No known substance compacts in such a way as to form a series of identically shaped tubes.

These finds are just as mysterious as their Precambrian counterparts in South Africa. The chalk strata in which they were discovered dates back sixty-five million years. This means the tubes were laid down towards the end of the Cretaceous period, contemporary with the last of the dinosaurs.

The scientists involved in the find, Y. Druet and H. Salfati, were utterly stunned by what they had discovered. They considered and abandoned several hypotheses before concluding the tubes had to be evidence of intelligent life. If they are right—and it is difficult to fault their conclusion—we need to ask where such intelligent life came from.

All fossil evidence points to the fact that the saurians were the dominant life form on our planet for almost 200 million years. There was simply no room for serious competition. Could the dinosaurs themselves have evolved an intelligent strain in that time? It is actually possible, if unlikely. Spielberg suggested the speedy raptors of Jurassic Park were clever enough to turn door handles, and scientists would not absolutely deny this could have been the case. But metallic tubes do not just signify intelligence, they indicate an advanced technology and this is completely out of court for the saurians.

We have already examined the question of extraterrestrial visitors in relation to the Precambrian finds. Once again the possibility of an extraterrestrial visit in the Cretaceous cannot be absolutely ruled out, but once again the remaining Mesozoic finds clearly point to human involvement. So, on balance we might be justified in claiming the tubes found by Druet and Salfati were spare parts for a time machine.

Such speculation, wild though it seems, is borne out by one of the most remarkable discoveries ever made. According to Dr. W. H. Ballou,[3] geologist John T. Reid was prospecting for fossils in Nevada in 1922 when, like William J. Meister in Utah, he stumbled on a fossil shoe print. Or, to be strictly accurate, he stumbled on what appeared to be the petrified remains of part of a leather sole.

The front part of the sole was missing, but a good two-thirds remained. These showed the thread marks where the welt had originally been joined and an indentation where the heel of the shoe's owner would have produced wear.

Reid brought his find to a photographer who took pictures magnified twenty times. These clearly showed the twist and warp of the thread and also brought up what appeared to be a line of stitch perforations running parallel to the rim.

The fossil was shown to Professors H. F. Osborn, W. D. Matthew, and E. O. Hovey of the American Museum of Natural History all of whom agreed it dated from the Triassic period, but since it could not possibly be what it appeared to be, they concluded they were examining a freak of nature which, by an incredible coincidence, mimicked the sole of a modern shoe. Dr. James F. Kemp, a geologist at Columbia University, reached essentially the same conclusions, both about the dating and the nature of the object.

Shoe manufacturers (unnamed) who examined the find were less reticent than the geologists. They stated categorically they were looking at the remnants of a hand-welted sole. If they were right, then once again the extra terrestrial hypothesis becomes untenable. We are looking at an undeniably human artifact, but one dated to a time long before humanity had evolved on the planet. It begins to look as if a Time Safari customer lost the sole of his handmade shoe while scrabbling over rough ground looking for his dinosaur.

If the Nevada time traveler was looking for his dinosaur, there is evidence that one of his colleagues actually found one in the Turkmen Republic of the former USSR. In 1983, the Moscow News carried a short report of a human footprint imbedded in Jurassic rock strata. No details were given except that the find had been examined by Professor Amanniyazov of the Turkmen Academy of Sciences, who was only prepared to state that it "resembled" a human footprint. The professor's reticence may be explained by the fact that this print was found beside another made by a three-toed dinosaur.

While the evidence continues to mount, we are still some way from showing time travel to be even theoretically possible. Falling through a Black Hole might do the trick, but if we are brutally honest, we have to admit there are no guarantees.

First, of course, you need to reach your Black Hole. The nearest is more than ten light-years away. Even assuming your technology allows you to travel at, or near, the speed of light (no technology allows you to travel faster) your round trip will take a minimum of twenty years, plus whatever time you spend rummaging around in the copy of your past. Twenty years is a long time to lose out of a human life span, but there is another point to consider. Because you made the trip near light speed, you would experience the time dilation effect predicted by Einstein—remember our discussion of the Twins Paradox? You would return to an Earth where your friends and family were all long dead, where society itself had moved on, where you would be unfamiliar with current technology, where your very trip would be little more than a footnote in the history books. This is a huge price to pay even for time travel.

If, however, you are prepared to pay it, you next have to solve the gravitational problem. This is, as I have already pointed out, a technical problem, but a technical problem of such magnitude that we do not have the slightest idea of how to tackle it, even in theory.

Should the miracle happen and scientists develop their version of Cavourite, the anti-gravity screen postulated by H. G. Wells, you still do not know if you are entering the ultimate time machine or not. For all their predictions, physicists still have to contend with the singularity—indeed, many of their predictions are based on the assumption that the singularity exists in nature and is not, like the cartography singularity, an aberration of viewpoint. You lose both ways. If the singularity does not exist in the real world, then the possibility of the Black Hole being a time machine diminishes dramatically. If it does, then no scientist can really tell you what it means in practical terms. Every description you have ever read about what happens in a Black Hole is no more than a physicist's guess. The best of them admit it's not even likely to be a good guess.

Finally, if you are prepared to bet your life, you still have to survive the experience. I know of no sane underwriter who would give you any odds at all of doing so. For the prospective time traveler, Black Holes are a very poor bet.

Fortunately, there are indications they may not be needed.

More than thirty years after Einstein's publication of his General Theory of Relativity, the logician Kurt Gödel showed the equations permitted journeys through time in certain rare circumstances. This was not just another version of the time dilation effect—Gödel was clear that the direction of travel could be into the past. More to the point, it could reach beyond your personal timeline. You could, in short, investigate history like Marty McFly in *Back to the Future*.

"By making a round trip in a rocket ship in a sufficiently wide curve," Gödel said, "it is possible in these worlds to travel into any region of the past, present and future and back again."[4]

Gödel himself was very wary of his own theory. He is on record as saying, "This state of affairs seems to imply an absurdity, for it enables one ... to travel back into the near past of those places where he himself has lived. There he would find a person who would be himself at some earlier period of his life. Now he could do something to this person which, by his memory, he knows has not happened to him."[5]

This was Gödel's version of the Grandfather Paradox with a far less gruesome emphasis, but like the cartographic singularity, the problem may be little more than viewpoint. Certainly, the fact that a theory implies an absurdity is no reason to dismiss it. Newton's theories implied the absurdity of action at a distance. Special Relativity gave us the absurdity of time dilation. A far more serious objection to Gödel's work is that the model he discovered bore no resemblance to the world we live in. It was, in other words, a theoretical construct which, while possible in that it broke no laws of physics, depended on situations and configurations that simply do not arise in reality as we know it. It is obviously unsafe to dismiss any theory, however wild, which conforms with the mathematical basis of modern physics. It is equally obvious that Gödel's approach will not give us time travel on demand.

Another implication of General Relativity looks altogether more promising. This is the concept of a wormhole. As used by the physicist John Wheeler, who was the first to see this implication, a wormhole is a very peculiar type of tube which connects what would otherwise be distant parts of the universe ... or different times of the universe. True to the Minowski equations, a wormhole means you can travel in space, but not in time, or travel in time but not in space.

Like the first postulates of Black Holes, wormholes are currently theoretical features of space-time. Nobody has actually discovered one just beyond the orbit of Mars, or lurking in a sparsely populated area of New York State. Unless, of course, it was a wormhole that briefly connected South America and the Philippines in the late sixteenth century.

On October 24, 1593, a Spanish soldier reported for guard duty at the palace in Mexico City. He seemed ill at ease and confused. More to the point, he was improperly dressed. His uniform, while obviously military, was not that of the palace guards.

The authorities hauled him away for interrogation. The man quickly admitted he was not sure where he was. He thought he had somehow lost his way while walking to the palace, but it soon transpired the palace he was looking for was not in Mexico City. He had been ordered to report for duty at the palace of Manila on the Philippines.

Worse was to come. The man insisted he had been stationed in Manila and that he had received his orders there that very morning. He added that the Spanish Governor of the Philippines had been killed the night before. When he was told he was now in South America, he shook his head in disbelief.

These were the days when the sea journey from Manila to Mexico took several weeks. There was no way the man could have been in the Philippines one morning and in Mexico City the same afternoon. Since he was obviously lying, the military authorities locked him up.

He remained locked up for two months. Then, a ship from the Philippines confirmed that the Governor was indeed dead—murdered on the night before the soldier turned up so mysteriously in Mexico. The man was released and subsequently returned to his billet in Manila.

There are a great many case histories of this type, although most of them chronicle unlikely disappearances without a subsequent reappearance elsewhere. For example, the so-called "Dragon's Triangle" south of Japan officially claimed 1,472 small ships (under two thousand tons) from 1968 to 1972. Since 1949, the official tally of major ships lost in the area is forty. In March of 1957, three planes disappeared within two weeks in this area.

Many of these losses have perfectly natural explanations, but many more defy logic. Between 1949 and 1954, ten large ships vanished taking hundreds of crewmen with them and leaving no trace whatsoever. In 1942, an Imperial Japanese Navy task force consisting of three destroyers and two aircraft carriers disappeared. There is no allied report indicating these vessels were lost to enemy action.

This sort of case history tends to be categorized as Earth Mysteries (or, worse still, Fortean) in published sources and does not form part of the required reading for any self-respecting physicist. This is a pity since manifestations of things as weird as wormholes are likely to produce weird effects. So long as scientists assume the consequences of their most bizarre theories must somehow be confined to the distant reaches of the galaxy, they are unlikely to find confirmation of them closer at hand.

Physicists may perhaps be forgiven for his sort of blind spot where wormholes are concerned, since there have been some theoretical problems associated with their existence. When you examine the concept of the wormhole from the Newtonian or even the Einsteinian perspective, your calculations will show you that in practical terms they are tubes leading nowhere. The problem is a Newtonian wormhole can exist for such a short time that entering it would be impossible, and, if you were somehow enabled to do so, the structure would collapse before you could get anywhere through it. Neither Special nor General Relativity formulae make one whit of difference to this characteristic. If wormholes exist, the calculations indicate they exist for only a fraction of a second.

There are, however, at least three respected scientists—the cosmologists Michael Morris, Kip Thorne, and Ulvi Yurtsever—who think some wormholes, perhaps even many wormholes, may exist long enough to be useful. They reached this conclusion by introducing into their calculations the eerie findings of quantum physics.

Endnotes

1. The supercontinent from which Africa, South America, Australia, Antarctica, and India split off between 190 and 135 million years ago.

2. Or perhaps they already have.

3. Article, "Mystery of the Petrified 'Shoe Sole' 5,000,000 Years Old" in the *New York Sunday Times* American edition of October 8, 1922.

4. Quoted by Coveny and Highfield in *The Arrow of Time*.

5. Ibid.

CHAPTER FIFTEEN

Quantum physics came into being for much the same reason as the Special Theory of Relativity: Einstein noticed a peculiarity about light. In this instance, Einstein didn't make the great leap forward on his own. He was building on the work of a German physicist called Max Planck. Planck, in turn, had been wrestling with a particularly knotty problem related to what was called black body radiation. This, in turn, was to have implications for our understanding of the behavior of the atom.

It's difficult to believe that when I was at school, atoms were simple things, invented, as I recall, by the Greeks. As explained to me, if you got a lump of matter—like a brick—and cut it in half, you were left with two smaller bits of the original. If you then took one of those bits and cut it in half, you got two more bits that were even smaller. If you kept cutting the brick in half, the bits would keep getting smaller and smaller until you would need a microscope to see what you were doing. Eventually you would end up with a bit that was just too small to cut in half. This bit was the atom, a piece of matter so small you couldn't divide it any more.[1]

The history of atomic thought is sort of interesting. It goes back to 500 B.C. when Leucippus and Democritus, a brace of philosophers from the Aegean seaport Abdera, came to the conclusion that everything was made up of tiny invisible bodies they called atomos (which means indivisible). They believed that atoms and space were the only ultimate realities. Everything, but everything, was made up of just these two things.

Aristotle and Plato soon contradicted what my teachers told me by suggesting you could keep on chopping the brick forever. You simply would not reach a stage where it would no longer subdivide.

Because of the immense prestige of these two great thinkers, this viewpoint was accepted for millennia. It only really started to be questioned at the beginning of the nineteenth century when experimental science was overtaking pure thought as the royal road to truth. A British chemist named John Dalton came to the conclusion that the existence of atoms would go some way towards explaining certain chemical reactions and the behavior of gases. He defined an atom as the smallest indivisible unit of matter that still retained its chemical properties.[2]

Dalton's ideas weren't taken up all that quickly. While his chemical colleagues recognized the concept of atoms was useful, they did not necessarily accept that atoms actually existed in the real world. Eventually, the evidence became overwhelming. What really cracked it was something called Brownian motion. Get out your trusty microscope and take a look at a drop of water. If there are any pollen, dust, or soot particles suspended in there, you can watch them dance around. This is Brownian motion. But what makes them dance? According to Einstein in 1905, they are colliding at random with the invisible water molecules that surround them.

Having decided atoms really existed, the physicists were then faced with the problem of what they looked like, how they functioned: in short, the problem of atomic structure.

Ernest Rutherford, of the University of Manchester in England, was the first to tell us. With his colleagues Hans Geiger[3] and Ernest Marsden, he bombarded gold foil with beams of alpha particles using radioactive material and measured the result. To their astonishment, the occasional particle bounced instead of passing straight through—a situation analogous, in Rutherford's own words, to firing a fifteen-inch naval shell at tissue paper and finding it was coming right back at you.

Alpha particles have a positive electrical charge. Rutherford reckoned the only thing that would bounce them back that way was something else with a positive electrical charge. He came to the conclusion that gold atoms had to have a positively charged core.

Rutherford's critical gold foil experiment was carried out in 1909. The following year he celebrated Christmas by announcing his theory of atomic structure. As he saw it, the atom was largely empty space. At the center of this space was the positively charged nucleus—the largest hunk of stuff in the entire atom. Orbiting around it were particles called electrons which, unlike the nucleus, had a negative electrical charge. In other words, as Rutherford saw it, the atom was like a little solar system: the nucleus equated with the sun, the electrons were the planets.

Although nobody remarked on it at the time, this model of the atom was a revival of a very old idea indeed: the Hermetic notion of a microcosm that reflects in miniature the structure of the macrocosm. It proved as popular in modern times as it had in the ancient world. It was the model of the atom taught to me by the same teacher who explained you got to atoms in the first place by chopping up a brick. But Rutherford's microcosm was almost unimaginably small. To get an idea of scale, you need to see the nucleus as having a radius of 1/1,000,000,000,000,000th of a meter. The nucleus, you will recall, is the biggest bit of the atom. Nobody even attempts to tell you what an electron measures, only that it orbits the nucleus at a distance of about 1/100,000,000,000,000th of a meter. This orbit defines the outer limit of the atom. If you are visualizing it all properly, you will see that 999,999,999,999,999/1,000,000,000,000,000ths of your average atom is empty space.

Rutherford's model looked good to begin with, but after a while its limitations began to show. What showed them up was radioactivity. Radioactivity was thought of in those days as the spontaneous emission of particles from certain elements. It soon became obvious the only place the particles could come from was inside the nucleus. This suggested that if you could crack open the nucleus, you would find another, even smaller, structure inside. But you couldn't crack open the nucleus—remember the Greeks and my brick: the atom was actually defined as uncrackable.

All the same, Rutherford's model looked very good as far as it went. Physicists started to apply Newtonian rules to the electrons in order to predict how they would behave in their orbits and quickly got into big trouble. Once the calculations were complete, it became clear that if electrons emitted light in the way Newtonian physics predicted, they would quickly radiate off all their energy and spiral down to collide with the nucleus like a planet falling into the sun. It was a worrisome time for physicists. If atoms were as unstable as their calculations suggested, it meant that anything made from atoms (which meant everything there was, including the physicists themselves) was liable to fall apart at any moment.

About a decade before the scientists started seriously to worry about falling apart, Max Planck was wrestling with the mystery of the relationship between the temperature of a body and the amount of radiation it emits. Radiation emission changes dramatically with temperature. A warm poker hardly radiates at all and looks black. Heat it in the fire and it starts to radiate, glowing red. Heat it a lot more and its radiation pattern changes so it glows white.

To try to understand the relationship between these various changes, physicists had abandoned the real world with all its imperfections for an ideal world in which there existed a perfect material for the emission and absorption of radiation. They called this material a "black body." It didn't exist in reality, but it was a useful concept around which to construct a theory of radiation. Inevitably, the radiation they theorized about came to be called "black body radiation."

The first theory that emerged out of black body radiation was a bit of a curate's egg. As long as you were talking about the low frequency end of the spectrum, the reds and the infrareds, it worked well enough. You could check your figures by experimentation, and they agreed fine. When you applied it to the high end, the figures showed the radiation should be infinite. If this had happened inside a Black Hole, they would have called it a singularity. As it was, the nineteenth-century physicists called it the ultraviolet catastrophe and tried to forget it. They knew it was nonsense. Their observations already showed them heated bodies didn't give off anything remotely resembling infinite quantities of radiation in the ultraviolet spectrum. In fact, high frequency radiation was about as low-key as low-frequency radiation. The peak actually came somewhere in the middle.

In 1900, Max Planck reluctantly came up with a theory that worked. Reluctantly because he was one of the physicists in those days who didn't believe in atoms. He was right there with Aristotle and Plato in thinking you could cut the brick indefinitely. To his great embarrassment, the theory that worked for black body radiation—and worked beautifully—was based on the reality of atoms.

This wasn't the worst of his embarrassment. In order to start making his calculations, Planck had to assume something pretty silly. He had to assume, against all common sense, that atoms would emit radiation in bursts, not in a continuous stream. In other words, what looked like a constant beam of radiation was really a little burst of energy, followed by another little burst of energy, followed by another, *ad infinitum*—or at least as long as the energy lasted.

As if that wasn't bad enough, he discovered that these packets of energy were of specific sizes. You couldn't just hack an energy beam into as many packets as you wanted. The number and size of the packets were predetermined, were, in other words, inherent in the nature of radiation. Radiation, whether you liked it or not, came in little specific packets, and there was nothing you could do about it. Out of this insight came something called Planck's constant, another one of nature's fundamental values like the speed of light. If you know Planck's constant, then all you have to do is multiply your frequency by it in order to find the amount of radiated energy. This works wonderfully at low, middle, and high ends of the spectrum. In one bound, you (with the aid of Max Planck) have solved the puzzle of black body radiation.

Planck called each packet of energy a quantum, plural quanta. He didn't know it at the time, but he had just helped the birth of a whole new ball game, quantum physics.

He was a reluctant midwife. His problem was that he didn't want to face the implications of his discovery. He kept pretending it was just a convenient way of looking at things, not a description of literal reality. Einstein was more courageous. He saw the implications all too well, faced them squarely, and won a Nobel Prize for his pains. Most people imagine Einstein's Nobel Prize for Physics was earned by one or both his Theories of Relativity, but it wasn't. He got it (in 1921) for work he did in 1905 on a phenomenon called the photoelectric effect. This is the term for a curious bit of weirdness that occurs when you shine light on metal. Light is, of course, a stream of particles called photons. When they hit the metal—with the speed of light—they gouge out a few electrons. The number of electrons released depends on the intensity of the light while the energy of the electrons depends on its color. What you're looking at here is an interaction between light and matter that couldn't be explained by classical physics. Einstein explained this by extending Planck's idea. He suggested black body radiation wasn't the only thing to come in packets—light did too. Within a decade or so, experimentation showed he was right.

In 1913, a Danish physicist named Nils Bohr had the bright idea of applying the new rules of quantum mechanics to Rutherford's atom. They worked beautifully. A juggernaut has started to roll and it was only a matter of time before somebody came up with a fully fledged quantum theory.

That somebody proved to be two somebodies. One was a German physicist with hay fever named Walter Heisenberg. He was recovering from an attack in the pollen-free atmosphere of Heligoland in the North Sea when he created his theory of "matrix mechanics," the world's first consistent formulation of quantum theory. And a weird formulation it was. In algebra, a multiplied by b is the same as b multiplied by a, another way of saying 3 x 4 is the same as 4 x 3. In matrix mechanics it isn't. I know it doesn't make sense, but blame Heisenberg. He was saying—and other scientists have since noticed he was right—that the order in which you measure things in the subatomic world makes a difference to the final result.

The other somebody was an Austrian physicist with marriage problems named Erwin Schrödinger. He was ensconced with his mistress in the Swiss Alps when he created a theory of wave mechanics which described the same thing as Heisenberg's matrix mechanics from a different viewpoint. The birth of quantum physics, a whole new way of looking at the subatomic world, was complete.

Endnotes

1. I was vastly irritated as a child when I learned that somebody actually had split the atom. Since atoms were, by definition, indivisible, splitting one seemed illogical to the point of wickedness.

2. What we would now call a molecule, except that molecules can certainly be divided further into what we now call atoms.

3. Who subsequently invented the now-famous geiger counter which detects radioactivity.

CHAPTER SIXTEEN

There is a fundamental experiment in quantum physics that produced results so paradoxical it has transformed our view of the world into something fantastic. Even time travel seems conventional by contrast. The experiment, briefly stated, is this:

A beam of subatomic particles is directed towards a sensitized surface that will register its impact. A screen is then placed between the source of the particles and the sensitized surface. There are two slits in the screen through which particles can pass—the screen otherwise blocks them. Each of the two slits can be opened and closed independently by the experimenter.

Subatomic particles, as their name implies, were once thought of as very tiny cannon balls. Common sense—and Newtonian physics, if you still insist on using Newton's findings—suggest that if both slits are opened, twice as many of these little cannon balls will get through than if you only open one. The reality is that more particles get through if only one slit is opened.

You can conduct the same experiment using light. Shine a light through a slit in a card and you will get an area of light on any screen beyond it. Make two slits and you will get two areas of light. Where they overlap you will get alternating dark and light bands on the screen—an interference pattern. But light, as you know, is a stream of particles called photons. If you reduce your light source right down so that it releases only a single photon, you would expect it to go through one pinhole or the other if both are open. However, when the two slits are open, the single photon doesn't land anywhere within the area of the interference pattern produced by having two slits open. Repeat the experiment a few times and the *individual* photons start to build up an interference pattern exactly as if they were a photon stream. What's even worse, you *don't* get the pattern when just one slit is open. So added to the question of how a single photon manages to interfere with itself (or interfere with other photons that landed earlier or were going to be sent through later), you have to ask how it knows when two slits are open and not just one. Einstein, who was highly suspicious of quantum physics all his life once remarked sourly that the photon must be telepathic.

Other scientists wrestled more seriously with the dilemma. To make sense of the findings, they began to postulate that subatomic particles were not particles at all, but wave forms. Nobody knows what the subatomic world looks like from direct observation: there are no instruments available that will reveal its mysteries. Physicists create models of this world in relation to the results of their experiments. So, they started out with a model of subatomic particles as little cannon balls, then amended the model in the face of experiments like the one just described, to a model of particles that were actually wave forms.

There is nothing mysterious or difficult about a wave form. You can picture it like a wave on the sea. It goes up and down and travels forward.

As you visualize a wave form, it is easy to see that, unlike a simple particle (unlike a little cannonball in other words) a wave could pass through both slits simultaneously. This meant that you would expect to find no more hits registering on the sensitive surface when two slits are open than when you only open one. All that happens is each wave splits to get through the slits, then reforms on the other side. Indeed, since a percentage of these split waves will collide (thus canceling each other out) fewer waves will actually get through two slits than would get through one—exactly what the experimental findings showed.

Wave theory seemed to solve the mystery, except for one important point. The particles, which behaved like waves while passing through the two slits in the screen, promptly turned back into particles immediately afterwards. A wave striking the sensitized surface would naturally strike it all at once, like a sea wave breaking on a beach, but the experiment showed this does not happen. The particles strike in specific locations—like little cannonballs.

Physicists started to refer to wave-particle duality (which named the behavior, but did not explain it) and lived for years with the uneasy knowledge that particles behaved like particles in certain circumstances and like waves in others. It is important to appreciate that the wave-particle duality works—that is to say, by considering subatomic particles in this way, scientists have been able to predict accurately the behavior of these particles across a whole range of situations. In other words, the duality is real—it just fails to make much sense.

It made so little sense, in fact, that physicists began to wonder if the wave existed in the objective world at all. They theorized that it might actually be a mental convenience that enabled them to keep track of what they were seeing, another example of the organizing function of the human mind.

So, physicists started to think the whole wave-particle duality was actually part of their own organizing function. The wave was really a collection of possibilities that behaved in a wave-like manner. In other words, the basic particle was still a little cannonball, but instead of simply observing the behavior of this little cannonball, you took account of all the various things that could happen to a little cannonball—all its probabilities, in other words—and your mind organized them into a wave-like structure. Quantum particles began to be seen increasingly as probability waves.

Physicists are intelligent and often subtle people, and this sort of thinking is not particularly easy for the rest of us to follow. If you apply it to the troublesome double-slit experiment, you can see its attraction. Given the concept of the probability wave, you can return to the comforting picture of particles as little cannonballs. As each little cannonball approaches the two open slits in the screen, the probability wave (which really only exists in the mind of the observer) represents the different possibilities open to the particle—in essence whether it passes through the top slit or the bottom slit, or strikes the screen and is absorbed or deflected. The probability wave did not predict precisely where the particle would go, only where it was most likely to go.

Probability waves worked just as well to predict results as did the original concept of physical wave form particles. Furthermore, it was very easy to see that the probabilities were bound to change from a situation where one slit was opened, to a situation where you opened two. The theory of probability waves neatly explained particle behavior, but left one niggling problem. If particle waves were actually probability waves and probability waves were actually an organizing function in the mind of the scientist, how on earth did you explain the observable fact that probabilities somehow managed to interfere with one another exactly like physical wave forms?

In 1957, a young American physicist named Hugh Everett III came up with the answer in the course of his doctoral work at Princeton University. In an argument of almost blinding simplicity, he suggested that if two probabilities can interfere with one another, each of them must have an actual existence. But since there is no way both probabilities can exist in our universe, it follows logically that there must be a second, parallel universe to house the second probability.

The implications of the Everett theory are quite bizarre. They involve an ongoing interaction of the two parallel universes, which split and merge continually in relation to specific events. In the famous double slit experiment, the splitting of the two universes produces the wave-like behavior, while the merging gives us back our little cannonball particle.

Here, of course, we have come back full circle to the parallel universes that relativity theory suggests are found in Black Holes. While the nearest Black Hole is light-years distant from the Earth and would rip you apart if you were silly enough to come near it, Everett's parallel universes seem to be accessible right here on our home planet. Indeed, in the multitude of choices you make throughout your life, you would, quite naturally, be weaving in and out of them all the time.

It was this sort of thing that left Einstein disgusted with quantum physics—he once said he simply couldn't believe the entire universe would change just because a mouse looked at it, but increasing numbers of physicists are taking Everett's ideas seriously. The reason for this is that wild though the theory of a multiverse sounds, the alternative theory is even worse. The alternative theory—which used to be the classical theory of quantum physics—

is that the act of observation causes the probability waveform to collapse into a single actuality.

That doesn't sound too bad while you're talking about particles hurtling through slits, but it gets very messy on the larger scale. When you reach the world of cabbages and kings, you generate paradoxes like that of Schrödinger's Cat, which is held to be both alive and dead until the moment the scientist opens the box to see whether or not it was poisoned. On the cosmic scale, you have to go even farther and ask what observer collapses the probability waves that determine stars going into nova and galaxies colliding. The religiously minded might answer that the ultimate observer must be God, but to physicists, God is just a name given to the final unknown and is hence an admission of defeat. Bringing God into your equations is like finding a singularity—a sign that your theory just broke down.

So, it now looks as though both great postulates of modern physics, relativity and quantum mechanics, have given us the marvels of multiple space-time continua, the theoretical possibility of accessing them, and the certainty that if you can slip sideways, so to speak, in space, you can certainly slip sideways in time.

CHAPTER SEVENTEEN

How do you decide whether tomorrow's technology includes time travel? Where do you look for evidence that our descendants have discovered the means of temporal voyaging? If time travel is a one-way process forward, there is no way we can know. If, as the new physics suggests, it is possible to move back in time, then the evidence we are searching for will present itself as anachronisms. Human beings are careless. They drop things they shouldn't, like the metal tubes found at Saint-Jean de Livet in France. They are also vulnerable. Whatever safeguards are in place, sooner or later someone will be trapped in a time period other than their own and die there. If the time period is historical, their death will leave no anachronistic trace, but if we examine the depths of prehistory, it becomes possible to trace the series of temporal disasters which left a trail of corpses where they decidedly should not be.

The evolutionary process of our species has now been well charted. Experts assure us that the earliest true humans (members of the genus *Homo* including the now-extinct human species *Homo habilis* and *Homo erectus*) appeared close to the end of the Pliocene Epoch, about two to three million years ago. Most of human evolution therefore occurred during the Pleistocene, which stretches from about two and a half million years ago to the present. Thus, if you find human remains substantially earlier than this period, you know something is wrong. If you find human remains which exhibit modern characteristics—which is to say remains of *Homo sapiens sapiens*—you know something is badly wrong. Such remains suggest an anachronism.

In the late summer of 1860, the geologist Professor Guiseppe Ragazzoni of the Technical Institute of Brescia, Italy, was collecting fossil shells in Pliocene strata of the Colle de Vento, a low hill near Castenedolo when he discovered several human bones and the top portion of a human cranium. He showed his finds to two fellow geologists who insisted they must be recent burials. The bones were obviously of an anatomically modern human, but their placement in the strata would have dated them somewhere between three and four million years—long before *Homo sapiens* evolved on the planet.

Despite the fact that the cranium portion had been completely filled with fossil coral and the blue-green clay characteristic of the hill's Middle Pliocene stratum, Ragazzoni allowed himself to be persuaded and threw the bones away as scientifically worthless.

All the same, he wondered. On his own admission, he could not get out of his mind the idea of a body washed ashore by the ancient sea that once lapped the southern shores of the Alps, then covered with coral, shells, and clay. Eventually, he gave in to the feeling and returned to the site. To his delight, he found more bone fragments in the same stratum. The theory of a recent burial was beginning to weaken.

Fifteen years later, Ragazzoni advised his friend Carlo Germani to buy a tract of land at Castenedolo. He thought Germani might make a comfortable income from it by selling the phosphate-rich clay to farmers as fertilizer. Mindful of his earlier finds, Ragazzoni asked Germani to keep an eye out for any human remains when he was excavating the clay. Germani promised to alert him if anything was discovered.

Four more years went by. Then, on January 2, 1880, Germani was excavating less than fifty feet from the spot where Ragazzoni had made his find when he unearthed a substantial cache of human bones. Once again they were located in the Middle Pliocene stratum between the coral bank and the blue-green clay. True to his promise, Germani left the bones in place and called Ragazzoni who personally removed them from the stratum with the help of his assistant Vincenzo Fracassi.

Only twenty-three days later, Germani turned up two further jaw fragments and some teeth, which he passed on to Ragazzoni. These so excited the professor that he returned personally to the site and began serious excavations of his own. They were entirely successful. The hoard was now so sizable that he realized he must be dealing with the remains of more than one individual. He also realized there was no longer any question of recent burial.

All of them (the finds) were completely covered with and penetrated by the clay and small fragments of coral and shells, which removed any suspicion that the bones were those of persons buried in graves and, on the contrary, confirmed the fact of their transport by the waves of the sea.

Early the following month came the most exciting discovery of all—a complete human skeleton. If there were any lingering doubts about the age of the finds, this one dismissed them. The skeleton showed indications of having moved with the stratum itself, proof positive that it was not a recent burial. The skull was in several pieces, but Ragazzoni had it expertly restored. The result was a cranium "indistinguishable from that of a modern woman."[1]

Geologists who examined the blue clay layer agreed that it belonged to the Middle Pliocene, which would make the finds between three and four million years old. The anatomist Professor Guiseppe Sergi of the University of Rome examined the remains and concluded they were of four individuals, an adult male, an adult female and two children. A family outing through time that went disastrously wrong? With its warm coral sea and towering mountains, the Castenedolo area of Italy must have been a delight in the Pliocene, but it retained its dangers. Or perhaps the family was abandoned because of a rare technical hitch, like the crash of a present-day airliner.

Of course, there is always the possibility that our paleoanthropologists have got it wrong and humanity—modern humanity, Homo sapiens sapiens—evolved earlier than is generally supposed—and in a different country, but the further back you go, the less likely this becomes. Eventually, as we have seen while considering other finds, it ceases to be even theoretically possible. The Castenedolo finds are, in fact, the most recent anomalous finds to be discovered. Others build a case that becomes increasingly watertight.

The bone in your upper arm is called a humerus (the famous "funny bone" of a thousand medical jokes). The influential American physical anthropologist William White Howells and his colleague Bryan Patterson discovered an ancient humerus in 1965 while excavating a site at Kanapoi in Kenya. The bone was discovered on the surface, but all its characteristics, including the degree of mineralization, agreed with the material they had been finding in the sediments. They concluded the bone had eroded out of them.

The sediments lay below a layer of volcanic rock which yielded a potassium-argon dating between 2.5 and 2.9 million years. [2] Comparison with other sites suggested the sediments themselves were between 4 and 4.5 million years old.

At that age, it became immediately important to decide where the humerus came from. Patterson and Howells quickly decided it did not belong to a gorilla or an orangutan. Other candidates were chimpanzees, Australopithecines[3] or humans. They made detailed measurements of each which ruled out the chimps and the hominids. Their find corresponded most closely to the mean measurement of human armbones and actually duplicated the measurements taken of several specific human samples.

Anthropologists Henry M. McHenry and Robert S. Corruccini of the University of California also examined the find, comparing its measurements with all species of anthropoid ape, three species of monkeys, and two fossil hominids. They found that of all their comparisons, the bone was most similar to the armbone of a modern Eskimo. It was, they said, "barely distinguishable from modern *Homo*."[4] Except, of course, that modern *Homo* wasn't about when the fossil was laid down. We are reminded of Bradbury's Time Safaris. Not everyone would wish to return to the age of the dinosaurs. Big-game hunting in Africa has been popular for centuries and a trip to the Pliocene would even defuse ecological concerns, but perhaps, as sometimes happens, the big game proved more dangerous than the hunter and a chastened traveler returned to the twenty-fifth century minus an arm.

Another collection of ancient bones—much too ancient to fit the picture of human evolution—was discovered in 1853 by Dr. H. H. Boyce at Clay Hill in El Dorado County, California. They included a scapula, clavicle and parts of the first, second and third ribs of a human skeleton. Boyce, who was a medical practitioner, had made a special study of anatomy and was in no doubt at all about what he had found. The problem was he had found it while sinking a shaft as part of a prospective mining operation.

The stratum from which the bones emerged was early Pliocene or late Miocene, making them in excess of five million years old.

These bones were not the only Californian finds of human remains in excess of five million years. In February 1886, a mine owner removed a human skull from a 130-foot-deep gravel layer at a mine on Bald Hill, near Angels Creek. The gravel lay close to bedrock and under several layers of volcanic material laid down in the Oligocene, Miocene, and Pliocene. This would give it an age of over five million years, with the possibility that it might be substantially older, perhaps as much as nine million years. The find caused a sensation, but was widely dismissed as a hoax. One theory was that it had been placed at the bottom of the shaft in rude good humor by a miner determined to confound the experts. If so, he managed to find an old skull for his joke—those who examined it agreed it was fossilised to a high degree. This does not necessarily denote great age, but it does mean the bone was at least several hundreds of years old.

Geologist George Becker reported that Clarence King, a noted geologist with the U. S. Geological Survey, O. C. Marsh, the paleontologist and former President of the National Academy of Sciences, and Harvey Putnam of the Peabody Museum at Harvard all examined the skull and were convinced of its authenticity and age.

If these finds were genuine, they mean people with all the characteristics of modern humanity were in California long before they had any evolutionary right to be. If they came from a distant future, something prevented their getting back alive. Their bodies and clothing rotted, their bones gradually fossilised and those that survived were covered by ever-deepening sedimentary layers awaiting their lucky discovery by a bewildered geologist. The very rarity of such finds actually argues towards their origins. If, against all odds, our picture of human evolution is so wildly awry that *Homo sapiens sapiens* was in place, in America, more than five million years ago, then we would expect to find evidence of tribal groupings, colonies of early humanity, not just isolated bones, but associated artifacts and signs of habitation. This has not happened. Instead, we are faced with no more than a skull and bones, leaving us to wonder about the occasional tourist who did not make it home.

Temporal tourism seems such an outlandish concept it is as well to try to put it in some sort of context. Little more than a century or two ago, Africa was the Dark Continent unknown to all but a handful of intrepid Victorian explorers. Australia was a penal colony. Japan was culturally isolated. The Middle Kingdom of China absolutely barred all foreigners. American settlers were still fighting the Indians. The very wealthy made the fashionable Grand Tour of Europe perhaps once in their lives. Everybody else stayed at home. At such a period in history, tourism as we know it now would have seemed just as outlandish as temporal tourism does today. What changed the picture was technology. It increased the wealth of developed nations and lowered the cost of travel. The type of person who might just have managed Brighton in my grandfather's day now flies out to the Bahamas. In two hundred, five hundred or, perhaps, five thousand years' time, it may be no more odd to board a craft that could carry you to nature's own Jurassic Park or any other period of time that took your fancy.

Certainly, the evidence for temporal exploration, if not perhaps temporal tourism, continues to mount despite attempts by the scientific establishment to discredit it, rebury it, or simply ignore it. There is, for example, no more than a passing reference in the scientific literature of the human skeleton found in Miocene strata at Midi de France in the late nineteenth century. We are told to treat the find cautiously. Small wonder. The placement means this example of humanity was alive and well in France somewhere between five million and twenty-five million years ago.

There are more details to be had of finds in the Missouri tunnel. The Placer County region is characterized by deep layering of ancient volcanic material. Two human bones, one a leg bone, were found beneath the lava. In 1989, researcher Stephen Bernath approached the California Division of Mines and Geology for information and was told that andesite deposits in the region had yielded a potassium-argon date of 8.7 million years.

California seems to have been a popular location for our suspected time travelers. On the first day of 1873, the President of the Boston Society of Natural History officially reported news of another anomalous Californian find made some years earlier.

This one was made by Captain David B. Akey, Commanding Officer of a California Volunteer Company. Akey was involved in a mining operation at Table Mountain in Tuolumne County when a complete human skeleton was discovered at a depth of about 200 feet in a layer of gravel close to bedrock. There was a petrified pine tree in the same layer, near the bones.

The gravel layer, which had a volcanic overlay, is somewhere between thirty-three and fifty-five million years old, placing the skeleton in the Miocene period at the very latest and possibly as far back as the Oligocene. (Interestingly, mastodon teeth were discovered in a different area of the same layer suggesting these animals may have appeared in North America earlier than is generally believed.) A skeleton of similar age was discovered only a few years later at Delémont in Switzerland. The clay layers from which it was exhumed were Eocene, giving it a date between thirty-eight and forty-five million years.

A vastly older skeleton was discovered in Macoupin County, Illinois, according to a report in *The Geologist*. The bones, of an adult male, were ninety feet below the surface of the earth in a layer of coal capped by two feet of slate. An interesting feature of the find was that the skeleton was coated with some hard, black glossy material (which may have formed as a chemical reaction with the coal itself).

Illinois coal dates to the Pennsylvanian era, a specifically North American dating that equates roughly to the latter half of the Carboniferous. This would make the Macoupin skeleton between 286 and 320 million years old—a particularly violent anachronism since it means that a representative of our species was exploring North America at a time before a single mammal had evolved, before even the dinosaurs appeared.

Endnotes

1. Ragazzoni's 1880 report of the discoveries, quoted by Cremo and Thompson in *Forbidden Archaeology*.

2. See "Archaeological Dating" in the Appendix for a description of the potassium-argon dating technique.

3. Australopithecines comprise a genus of extinct hominid (human like) fossils generally considered to be a possible evolutionary ancestor of modern humans.

4. Quoted by Cremo and Thompson in *Forbidden Archaeology*.

CHAPTER EIGHTEEN

Anachronisms in prehistory are easy to spot. A metal tube or a human skeleton in a coal seam clearly stands out as something that shouldn't be there. Historical anachronisms are more difficult. The skeleton of a time traveler who died in Sumeria would not appear significantly different from the skeleton of a Sumerian. Even a misplaced piece of jewelry would not necessarily stand out if archaeologists were lucky enough to discover it.

All the same, historical anachronisms do exist. One arose in 1936 when Wilhelm König, the German director of the Iraq Museum laboratory, described a newly discovered find in these words:

> "A vase-like vessel of light yellow clay, whose neck had been removed, contained a copper cylinder which was held firmly by asphalt. The vase was about 15 cm high the sheet copper cylindrical tube with bottom had a diameter of 26mm and was 9 cm long. In it, held by a kind of stopper of asphalt, was a completely oxidised iron rod, the top of which projected about 1 cm above the stopper and was covered by a yellowish gray, fully oxidised thin coating of a metal which looked like lead. The bottom end of the iron rod did not extend right to the bottom of the cylinder, on which was a layer of asphalt about 3 mm deep."

When the various parts were brought together and examined, König realized it was only necessary to add acid or alkaline liquid for the device to be transformed into an electrical element. In other words, it was a battery, but it was a battery that had been discovered in a Parthian village, which meant it had been manufactured no later than A.D. 226—and might have been constructed as long ago as 248 B.C. Dr. Arne Eggebrecht took the trouble of duplicating the artifact and added alkaline liquid in the form of grape juice. It generated a measured half volt of electricity.

Modern use of electricity dates back no farther than the nineteenth century. When Luigi Galvani's experiments with "animal electricity" were published in 1791, the Italian physicist Alessandro Giuseppe Antonio Anastasio Volta began experiments that led him to theorize animal tissue was not necessary for conduction of electricity. Proof of the theory was his invention, in 1800, of the so-called voltaic pile, believed to be the world's first battery. If this really was the world's first battery, what were the Parthians doing with one in A.D. 226?

A similar problem arises with the Antikythera Mechanism.

In 1900, a team of divers searching for sponges on a rocky ledge off the island of Antikythera (located to the northwest of Crete) came across the hull of an ancient ship. Investigation showed it was laden with statues. Later that year, the divers returned to the site of the shipwreck having deduced, correctly, that there might be more money to be made diving for the ship's treasure than sponges.

The operation took several months, but salvaged substantial numbers of bronze and marble statues along with a few other artifacts. All were taken to the National Archaeological Museum in Athens.

The cleaning and restoration of the statues preoccupied the museum staff for almost a year. It was not until May 1902 that the archaeologist Spyridon Stais finally got around to an examination of the artifacts. One of them, a heavily corroded piece of bronze, contained cog wheels.

The find aroused considerable controversy, but little was done about it until 1958 when a full-scale investigation and restoration was undertaken by Dr. Derek de Solla Price, Avalon Professor of the History of Science at Yale University. The basic features of the artifact slowly came to light. It seems originally to have consisted of a wooden box set with various dials and carrying inscriptions which included an astronomical calendar. Inside were some twenty cog wheels and a system of differential gears. X-ray photography carried out by the Greek Atomic Energy Commission in 1971 indicated an array of meshing gears. This mechanism was unmatched before the late sixteenth century when similar gearing finally found its way into a clock. Yet the case inscriptions made it clear the device had been made about 80 B.C. The artifact as a whole was more sophisticated still: it seems to have been a working model of the universe, or possibly just the solar system, designed to show various laws of motion in action.

You might argue that the Baghdad battery represents no more than an early, undeveloped discovery of an electrical application which was possibly a little more common in the ancient world than we realize. The remarkable skill shown by craftsmen in gold leaf as far back as Ancient Egypt has raised the suspicion that some primitive form of electro-plating may have been used. But the Antikythera Mechanism is in a different category entirely. Price wrote bluntly:

> "Nothing like this instrument is preserved elsewhere. Nothing comparable is known from any ancient scientific text or literary allusion. On the contrary, from all we know of science and technology in the Hellenistic Age, we should have felt that such a device could not exist."[1]

If such a device was not the product of contemporary technology, it must have been imported. But from where? As Price, an acknowledged expert in the field, rightly says, there is no hint of such technological sophistication anywhere in the world at that time. Was the Antikythera Mechanism carried to Ancient Crete from the future? Or, rather more likely, did a craftsman in the first century B.C. receive a little help and advice from a time traveler?

The theory of advice from a time traveler seems utterly outlandish when we first confront it. Yet nothing we have found in modern physics so far denies the theoretical possibility of time travel and prehistory seems to be peppered with sufficient anachronisms to allow some credence to the idea. Furthermore, certain texts found in Madrid in 1965 offer strong support for it.

The Madrid texts date from the late fifteenth century. It is important to realize they have been fully authenticated, both on internal evidence and by comparison with other texts of the same date. No scholarly controversy surrounds them, yet these texts contain accurate and detailed descriptions of exploding missiles, modern machinery, streamlining, and even a bicycle.

The first step toward the development of the bicycle was the invention of the celerifere, or wooden horse, in France in the 1790s. Because its front wheel was fixed, this vehicle could not be steered, and the rider propelled it by pushing his feet along the ground. Germany's Baron Karl von Drais introduced a steerable front wheel in 1817. In 1838, Kirkpatrick Macmillan, a Scottish blacksmith, made the first machine with pedals, which drove the rear wheel by means of cranks. On the velocipede, a French invention of the 1860s, the front wheel was pedal-driven and revolved once with each revolution of the pedals. The speed of the machine was dependent on the size of the front wheel: the larger the wheel, the faster the bicycle. The front wheel of the pennyfarthing—used from the 1870s—reached diameters of five feet and more, while the back wheel might be only one-quarter that size. With its seat mounted over the huge front wheel, the high-wheel was dangerously unstable, and its use on poor roads led to many bicycling accidents.

Each and every one of these developments was actually superseded in the bicycle design which appears in the Madrid texts four hundred years earlier. It has wheels of equal size—the basic prototype of the modern bicycle which did not appear until J. K. Stanley's safety model in 1885. Perhaps even more astounding, it has modern pedals and is chain-driven to the back wheel via a gearing mechanism. Professor Augusto Marinoni of the Università Cattolica, Milan, comments:

> "While they recognize the unmistakable nature of the machine, the few scholars who have examined the drawing are decidedly reluctant to admit its antiquity. Since the application of the chain drive to the bicycle goes back only to the end of the nineteenth century, they propose a dating ... within the early years of the present century. Such a hypothesis, however, collides with insurmountable difficulties."

The Madrid texts also contain a sketch of what looks suspiciously like a modern guided missile. It has stabilizing fins and shows evidence of streamlining. It is, in fact, a high explosive artillery shell, years ahead of its time. Two further fins jutting back from the pointed nose contain powder which ignites on impact. This is just one of many advanced weapons detailed in the texts. The range includes shrapnel (subsequently invented by the British general Henry Shrapnel in the early nineteenth century), breech-loading cannon, water-cooled gun barrels, rocket-propelled grenades, and a machine gun.

Bern Dibner, Director of the Burndy Library, Norwalk, Connecticut, remarks that the texts ...

> "... often read like a modern mail order catalogue that offers an ingenious tool or gadget for every conceivable purpose. (One) device. . . mechanizes the primitive techniques then used for forming wire by pulling it through dies ... (Another) looks remarkably like a modern lathe and is often mistaken for one. Actually its function is to bore holes in logs. (A) wood planer makes use of a set of adjustable clamps ... A set of threaded nuts raises the timber to permit the plane to trim the top surface ... About 1495 ... (the author of the texts produced) a shearing machine ... to cut the nap off woollen cloth—a process then carried out by shearmen with enormous scissors who had to crop the nap like a barber ... A roasting device ... utilizes the heat of the fire to turn the meat automatically. At a time when almost all cooking was done over an open fire, the design not only promised to liberate the cook, but provided evidence of the first known use of a true air-screw."[2]

The wonders go on and on. The manuscripts reveal their author explored virtually every field of science. They not only contain solutions to practical problems of the day—the grinding of lenses, for instance, and the construction of canals and fortifications—but also envision such future possibilities as flying machines and automation. His observations and experiments into the workings of nature include the stratification of rocks, the flow of water, the growth of plants, and the action of light. The mechanical devices that he sketched and described were also concerned with the transmission of energy.

The texts describe release mechanisms which automatically drop a load when it is lowered to its fullest extent, air and water turbines, mechanical looms. They detail the modern method of copper engraving at a time when the printing press had only just been invented and the most advanced way of making an impression was by woodcuts. They include complex three-dimensional forms of solid geometry. They reveal a sophisticated knowledge of optics (there is a design for a simple camera), of architecture, of hydraulics, of planetary astronomy and, above all, of engineering. One scholarly analysis of the texts indicates they include details of screws, keys, rivets, bearings, pins, axles, shafts, couplings, ropes, belts, chains, friction wheels, toothed wheels, flywheels, levers, connecting rods, click wheels, gears, ratchets, brakes, engaging and disengaging gearing, pipes, pistons, pump cylinders, valves, springs, cranks, cams, and pulleys.

This is a stunning list piling anachronism upon anachronism, especially as the author of the texts was the illegitimate son of a Florentine notary who bemoaned the fact he received only the most basic education in his childhood. Could this really be true? Would it not make much more sense to assume these incredible records were left by a time traveler?

Perhaps, but I have cheated in the presentation. We know the author of the Madrid texts was no time traveler. He was born on April 15, 1452, not far from Florence in Italy. His name was Leonardo da Vinci, acknowledged as the greatest painter the world has ever known.

The details of his life have been thoroughly investigated. His artistic talent revealed itself early. In 1469 he was apprenticed to Andrea Verrocchio, a leading Renaissance master and remained with him until at least 1476. He entered the painters' guild in 1472. In 1478, he was commissioned to paint an altarpiece for the Palazzo Vecchio in Florence. Three years later, he undertook to paint the Adoration of the Magi for the monastery of San Donato a Scopeto, but left Florence for Milan about 1482.

Leonardo then worked for Duke Lodovico Sforza in Milan for nearly eighteen years, painting portraits, designing festivals, and a plethora of other pusuits. He took up scientific fields as diverse as anatomy, biology, mathematics, and physics. During this period, he also completed one of his masterworks, *The Last Supper*.

With the fall of his patron to the French in 1499, Leonardo left Milan. He went to Mantua and Venice, then back to Florence. His stay there was interrupted by time spent working in central Italy as a map maker and military engineer for Cesare Borgia. Again in Florence in 1503, Leonardo undertook several highly significant artistic projects, including the Battle of Anghiari mural for the Town Hall, the portrait of Mona Lisa, and the lost *Leda and the Swan*.

Leonardo returned to Milan in June 1506, called there to work for the new French government. Except for a brief stay in Florence between 1507 and 1508, he remained in Milan for seven years. In 1513 he accompanied Pope Leo X's brother, Giuliano de Medici, to Rome, where he stayed for three years, increasingly absorbed in theoretical research. In 1516–17, Leonardo left Italy forever to become architectural advisor to King Francis I of France, who greatly admired him. Leonardo died at the age of sixty-seven on May 2, 1519, at Cloux, near Amboise, France.

There is not much room here to speculate that this towering genius may have been a visitor from a future age. If time travel was involved at all in his career, the most we could reasonably say is that he might just possibly have been advised by someone from an era other than his own. Yet, there is one peculiarity about the work of Leonardo da Vinci that has never been satisfactorily explained. His extensive notebooks were fluently, even artistically, handwritten—but backwards. You need to hold them up before a mirror to read them.

Why did Leonardo write like that? Some scholars suggest he wanted to keep his notes private, but a child of five could work out how to read mirror writing. Surely, if privacy was what he wanted, he would have devised a code or cipher and encrypted his work secure from prying eyes. Even that makes little sense since his notebooks are choc-a-bloc with detailed drawings which explain his "secrets" far more clearly than a thousand words.

It seems the great artist's custom of mirror writing must remain a mystery. Yet, it is a mystery eerily reminiscent of something we discussed in Chapter Thirteen: the idea of physicist Fred Alan Wolf that there are literal mirror worlds which give theoretical access to the future and the past.

Endnotes

1. Quoted in *Arthur C. Clarke's Mysterious World* by Simon Welfare and John Fairley, Fontana Books, London, 1982.

2. From *The Unknown Leonardo*, Bedini, Brizio, Brugnoli, Hutchinson of London, 1974.

CHAPTER NINETEEN

I t is all very well to point out that nothing in Newtonian physics, nothing in relativity theory, nothing in quantum mechanics precludes the possibility of time travel, but it's probably true to say they don't preclude the possibility of pink elephants either. That's a long way from saying pink elephants and time travel actually exist. So, far, our evidence for temporal voyaging has been circumstantial—artifacts and human remains in time periods where they had no business to be. Is there anything in the work of modern science to show something, however small and insignificant, actually, literally, definitely manages to travel through time?

In the very first chapter of this book, I told you Einstein showed the speed of light to be an absolute—nothing can exceed it—but two physicists, Gerald Feinberg and George Sudarshan, think I may have lied. Working independently in the mid 1960s, they realized the Theory of Relativity did not actually rule out something traveling faster than light. It only ruled out accelerating something until it traveled faster than light.

If that seems the same thing to you, remember how Einstein reached his conclusions about the speed of light. Special Relativity shows that the mass of a moving object increases with its acceleration. By the time you get it up to light speed, its mass is infinite. The only reason photons (light particles) get to move at the speed of light is that they don't have any mass to begin with.

So, you can't take something—like a spaceship or an astronaut—and push it beyond the speed of light, because that would mean it had a greater than infinite mass, which is obviously impossible, but Feinberg and Sudarshan did a little lateral thinking. Suppose, they said, you start from the other side of light speed, so to speak. Suppose you don't have to accelerate something up to and beyond 186,000 miles per second. Suppose it's already going at that speed or more. It's acceleration that adds the mass, not speed. Getting up to any given speed adds mass, but once you get there, you can cruise forever without adding any more.

This meant that, in theory, you could have something—say a new particle—that was born going faster than the speed of light. They named their new particle the tachyon, after the Greek word meaning swift. Their calculations showed a tachyon could never slow down to less than light speed: the speed of light remains an absolute barrier both ways.

Tachyons have some very strange properties. If they lose energy, they go faster instead of slower. If they lose all their energy, they go at infinite speed. This seems pretty weird, but it doesn't mean they can't exist. There are quite a few particles known to exist in modern physics that are just as weird. At the 1932 Copenhagen Conference on Nuclear Physics, for example, the scientists mounted a playlet based (very loosely!) on Goethe's Faust during which Gretchen entered singing:

> My rest-mass is zero
> My charge is the same
> You are my hero
> Neutrino's my name!

Faust was played by Wolfgang Pauli, one of the foremost nuclear physicists in the world. He was the focus of the humor on account of his prediction, two years earlier, of a new particle, the neutrino, with very curious properties—or, rather, lack of them.

It was, Pauli suggested, the most elusive of all particles, having virtually no characteristics at all—neither mass, electric charge, nor magnetic field. It was not subject to gravity, nor influenced by the electrical or magnetic fields of any other particles with which it came in contact. It was, in short, a sort of disembodied spin, and could pass through any solid body—even a planet—as if it were empty space. The only thing that could stop it was a head-on collision with another neutrino: and the chances of that happening were estimated at ten billion to one.

Long though these odds were, it seemed there were enough neutrinos about to ensure the occasional collision actually did occur. In 1956, scientists F. Reines and C. Cowan eventually detected one at the Atomic Energy Commission's nuclear reactor on the Savannah River. However Faustian his idea, Pauli proved justified: neutrinos definitely existed.

If tachyons also exist, they must have one property of enormous importance to our present thesis. They can travel backwards in time. According to the Special Theory of Relativity, all faster-than-light objects must have this property. To understand why takes us into one of the most difficult areas of modern physics—the visualization of space-time.

So far, I've used the term space-time only to remind you that since 1915 no physicist has been entitled to consider space and time as separate realities. But what does space-time look like? You are bound to have huge trouble with this question because, like me, you experience space as space and time as time. What you don't experience directly and have never experienced directly is space-time as a single unit.

Physicists, you'll be relieved to hear, have the same trouble. Most of them don't even try to visualize space-time: they use the word and make their calculations without really bothering. But those who do, turn to geometry.[1]

Visualize a triangle. This isn't difficult at all. If you look around the room you will probably see half a dozen examples of a triangle to help you along. I can see one now: a book leaning at an angle on a shelf, making a triangle with the shelf and the wall. Now, what's the difference between a space triangle (the thing you've just visualized) and a space-time triangle? The answer is that in a space triangle, all the legs are in real space while in a space-time triangle, one of the legs is in imaginary space. But imaginary space doesn't mean unreal space or non-existent space. Imaginary space is very real indeed. We experience it as time. We know from Einstein that the way we experience it is wrong. We know what we call time and what we call space are both parts of the same thing, but because we can't experience them that way, we have to try to imagine them that way. Hence time is imaginary space.

The interesting thing about this is that the mathematical relationship between the legs of a space-time triangle is the same as the mathematical relationship between the legs of an ordinary space triangle. The only difference is that in a space-time triangle, you make one of your measurements in imaginary space.

This is where things get a little batty because it is actually possible to measure the length of the imaginary leg of your triangle (the one we experience as time) using the same sort of yardstick you use to measure the other legs. Distance—ordinary physical distance—is no longer thought of by physicists in terms of feet and inches, or even centimeters and meters. For accuracy and convenience, it's related to that good old absolute, the speed of light. You hear astronomers using this sort of measure every day: they'll tell you a star is so many light-years away. That's a measure of distance, but it's also a measure of time—the time taken for light to cross the distance between you and the star. Measuring distance in terms of time isn't so odd when you start to think about it. You probably do it yourself—have you ever mentioned a friend who lives an hour outside London? In this case you are relating to the time it takes him to travel there by car, but the principle is exactly the same.

So, back with our space-time triangle, if you measure the imaginary spatial extension (time) in seconds, you should measure the other legs in light-seconds. The two are absolutely comparable, so you can figure the geometry of your space-time triangle by using the yardstick of light speed.

Some pretty exciting things come out of this space-time geometry. While you can't, in the real world, move in space without also moving in time, it's perfectly easy to move in time without moving in space. You're probably doing it right now, unless you're reading this book on a train. Moving in time is what we usually call sitting still, but however it feels, you aren't sitting still. You're traveling through imaginary space. What's more, you're moving through it at the speed of light.

Physicists use the space-time triangle to figure out the properties of certain particles. Photons, the particles which make up light, have no imaginary hypotenuse to their space-time triangle. Weird though it sounds, they spend no time at all in our world. So, how come we can see them? Relativity. They spend no time at all in our world from their own viewpoint. They stick around long enough from our viewpoint for us to react to them—which is just as well, otherwise we'd all be blind as moles.

If this seems far out, wait until you find what happens when you apply space-time geometry to tachyons. We do not experience imaginary space (we can only imagine it.) What we experience is real time, but a tachyon can't experience real time. It can only imagine it. What a tachyon experiences is the reality of the space we call imaginary space, and since it experiences imaginary space as a reality, it can move backwards and forwards in imaginary space just as easily as we can move backwards and forwards in real space. This means a tachyon can move backwards and forwards in time.

Thus, as Dr. Richard Morris remarks, "If beams of tachyons could be employed to transmit signals, it would be possible to send messages into the past."[2] He does not take the next creative, outlandish step of suggesting that if beams of tachyons could be employed to drive a craft, that craft would be a time machine.

Do tachyons actually exist? You would think something as peculiar as this particle would be even more difficult to detect than Pauli's neutrinos. Fortunately there is a chance of doing so by means of Cherenkov radiation.

Cherenkov radiation is emitted by any charged particle moving faster than the speed of light. As we've already seen, you can't accelerate anything to a speed greater than the speed of light, but that's the speed of light in a vacuum. In certain things, like a block of glass or plastic, the speed of light is reduced. If a charged particle is accelerated to a speed just a little less than the speed of light and then injected into a block of glass or plastic, its speed can exceed the speed of light in the block, and Cherenkov radiation is given off. It's a bit like the shock wave (sonic boom) produced by an aircraft breaking the sound barrier.

It's calculated that tachyons must spontaneously emit Cherenkov radiation, even in a vacuum. As we speak, physicists are hard at work trying to detect tachyons, by searching for suitable Cherenkov radiation and analyzing elementary-particle reactions. At the time I write, they still haven't found one. This is disappointing, since the existence of a tachyon would go a long way towards establishing the theoretical reality of time travel, but fortunately it's not critical. There are other particles that will do just as well—and they have already been detected.

Endnotes

1. For a fuller exposition of the following concepts, see Fred Alan Wolf's *Parallel Universes*.

2. In *The Nature of Reality*, Noonday Press, New York, 1988.

CHAPTER TWENTY

By 1931, the problems of the new physics had become acute. In an attempt to reconcile Einstein's relativity theory with Schrödinger's wave mechanics, Paul Dirac of Cambridge proposed that space was not really empty at all, but filled with negative electrons—this is, electrons displaying negative energy and mass.

What he was talking about was the substance of ghosts, something which existed, but was, by definition, virtually impossible to detect. Dirac labeled this negative particle the anti-electron and predicted it would be extremely short-lived, since there was a tendency for it to be annihilated in collision with a positive electron.

Had he not been a Nobel Prize-winning physicist, it is doubtful if the scientific community would have taken him seriously. Niels Bohr suggested the theory should be posted on the forest trees of Africa to fascinate elephants so they could be captured humanely. Nonetheless, within a year of publication, tracks in the bubble-chamber of the California Institute of Technology convinced physicist Carl D. Anderson that he had stumbled on a new type of electron, which he called a positron. The particle turned out to be identical in every way to Dirac's predicted anti-electron.

It was the opening of the floodgates. Within a relatively short period of years, physicists discovered anti-particles corresponding with every known particle. Eventually, Dr. Edward Teller, the scientist who, more than any other, made the hydrogen bomb possible, was constructing a broad theory of anti-matter, a whole negative universe which, if it came into contact with our (positive) cosmos would result in a gigantic explosion.

The concept was discussed within the scientific community, then introduced to the general public by the mischievous Dr. Harold P. Furth in the November 1956 edition of the *New Yorker:*

> *Well up beyond the tropostrata*
> *There is a region stark and stellar*
> *Where, on a streak of anti-matter,*

Lived Dr Edward Anti-Teller
Remote from Fusion's origin,
He lived unguessed and unawares
With all his anti-kith and kin,
And kept macassars on his chairs.
One morning, idling by the sea,
He spied a tin of monstrous girth
That bore three letters: A.E.C.
Out stepped a visitor from Earth.
Then, shouting gladly o'er the sands,
Met two who in their alien ways
Were like lentils. Their right hands
Clasped ... the rest was gamma rays.

Electrons are matter. Positrons are antimatter. After the discovery of the antiproton in 1955 and the antineutron a year later, it was concluded that an antiparticle exists for each subatomic particle. Antiparticles have the same basic properties (mass, spin, etc.) as ordinary particles, but have the opposite charge, which, in turn, changes certain other properties.

Examining the spectrum of objects can't show whether they're made of matter or anti-matter because photon particles, which make up light, are identical to their antiparticles. Since matter in distant parts of the universe can only be examined in this way, we don't actually know whether it's matter or anti-matter. Indeed, it's pure speculation how much of the universe is matter and how much anti-matter. What isn't speculation any more is the reality of anti-matter. We know the particles exist, so we know anti-matter exists.

The existence of anti-matter highlights what the physicists call *time reversal invariance*. Both seem to be part of the overall symmetry of space-time. We've already seen how much physicists love symmetry, which is a pointer towards the accuracy of a given theory. Though we didn't use the term, we've already come across time reversal invariance. It's the fancy way of saying time travel doesn't break the current laws of physics.

If some motion is possible according to the known physical laws, then the time-reversed motion is almost always possible. For example, it would be unusual to observe an egg broken on the floor collect itself and fly back into its shell, like a movie run backward, but according to physics, it isn't impossible, just very unlikely. Movies of simpler processes, however, such as a spinning top or a vibrating bell, appear nearly normal when run backward.

If natural laws show time reversal invariance, however, natural processes don't. This is because things get very complicated when you put a lot of particles together. Take the broken egg example. To get time reversal where the egg flies back together again, you'd have to reverse the speeds and directions of all the molecules. The complexity of this process means there's an extremely small likelihood of its happening. In practical terms, the likelihood is so small we can safely consider it impossible. Complex systems generally run one way in time and one way only.

On the subatomic level you have other things to worry about —the strong nuclear force that holds atomic nuclei together, for example, or the weak force responsible for radioactive decay of things like neutrons. Neutrons decay into protons, electrons, and antineutrinos. Time-reverse that and you get antineutrinos, electrons, and protons coming together to form neutrons. In order for the time-reversal to work, the energies of the incoming particles must be the same as those of the previous outgoing particles, and the velocities and spins of the particles must be reversed. This process is just about possible, but like the resurrected egg, not exactly likely.

All the same, experiments with elementary particles have tested time reversal invariance and it appears to be theoretically valid for all processes except the weak decay of particles called kaons, but we're still talking theory. What we really need is some indication of time travel actually happening, at whatever level. Is there somewhere, anywhere, that the physicists really see it?

It's possible (and rather fun) to chart events in space-time. Take something like a hundred-meter sprint. Assume the event begins with the athlete strolling to the starting blocks, then getting into place and waiting for the starting pistol, then running the race so vigorously that she collapses, exhausted, a few yards beyond the finishing tape.

An ordinary space chart of this event would be basic and boring. It would look something like Diagram A, where the whole thing is represented by a single line.

Diagram A: Space chart of race

Start   Finish

A space-time chart (Diagram B) is a lot more interesting. This chart recognizes the fact that our athlete can't move in space without also moving in time. The first leg of the chart shows the walk to the starting blocks. The angle here is quite steep since she's only walking, so you can think of her as moving more in time than in space. The second leg shows her waiting for the starting

Diagram B: Space-time chart of race

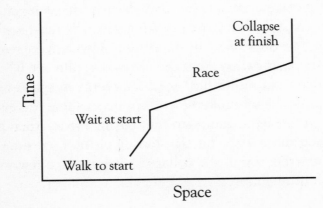

Time

Collapse
at finish

Race

Wait at start

Walk to start

Space

pistol. Now she's settled in the blocks, she isn't moving at all in space, but she continues to move in time. Once the race starts, she's moving fast in space, which slows her rate of movement in time, so the graph flattens out. Once she collapses at the finish line, she again stops moving in space, but continues, of course, to move in time. All neatly portrayed in our little chart.

Physicists don't spend time making space-time charts of races, but they do chart the behavior of particles in exactly this way. Take a look at the particle chart (Diagram C).

Diagram C: Space-time chart of particle

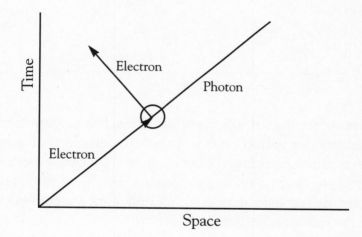

What you have here is an electron moving through space and time, minding its own business until, in the circled area, it emits a photon. In particle terms, this is like shooting off a rocket. As the photon speeds away, the backwards thrust of the rocket knocks the electron off course; so, instead of continuing on its original trajectory, it backtracks.

When properly drawn, this sort of space-time chart is far from my crude space-time representation of the race. The American physicist Richard Feynman noticed in 1949 that space-time diagrams of this sort correspond exactly with the mathematics of particle interaction. So, they're not just approximations—they're exact representations of the probabilities of what will happen.

Paul Dirac has assured us that should a particle contact its anti-particle, the result is mutual annihilation. The two disappear in a blinding flash of light. Diagram D is a Feynman diagram of just that very thing happening:

Diagram D: Space-time chart of particle/anti-particle collision

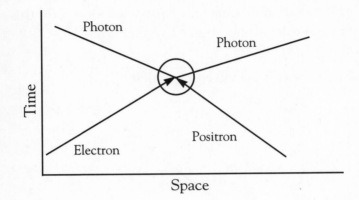

On your left, an electron traveling through space and time. On your right, a positron (which is the anti-particle of an electron) on a collision course. As the diagram shows, they meet in the circled area and annihilate each other, exactly as Dirac predicted. In the resultant explosion, two photons are emitted to provide the requisite flash of light.

At least, that's one way of looking at it. The big problem with subatomic events like this is that you can't be sure of anything. Not only can you not be sure of the outcome—according to Heisenberg's Uncertainty Principle, the best you can do is calculate the probabilities—but you can't even be really sure what you're looking at in the first place.

Take that first diagram of the electron knocking itself off course by emitting a photon. You might look at it and decide that wasn't what happened at all. What really happened, you might say, was that when the electron entered the circled area, it was suddenly annihilated. In the resultant explosion, a photon was created that whizzed off to the right at the speed of light, and so was a brand-new electron, which lumbered off to the left at a different speed than the original electron.

Now this might be no more than a fancy of yours, a quiet determination not to let the physicists have it all their own way, but there is nothing in the whole of quantum physics to say you're wrong. Your interpretation is absolutely valid. The diagram supports it, the maths support it. Every electron in the universe is absolutely identical to every other electron so there's no way of knowing whether the electron going left is the same electron as the original electron. It could, as you rightly say, be a brand-new electron.

This is not an academic point. Quantum physicists have decided that every subatomic event involves the annihilation of the original particles under observation and the creation of new ones. God alone knows whether this is really true, but by making the assumption, they can reach a consensus and by reaching a consensus they can enjoy the benefits of a consistent view of the subatomic universe. So, even though your idea of a particle exploding to produce another particle sounded most peculiar, consensus physicists would agree with you that that was what happened. Neither you nor the consensus could prove it, but it is consistent with the way they look on things in physics nowadays.

Let's apply that consensus view to our particle/anti-particle collision. Here's the diagram (Diagram E) again, with two small but very important changes:

Diagram E: Space-time chart of particle time travel

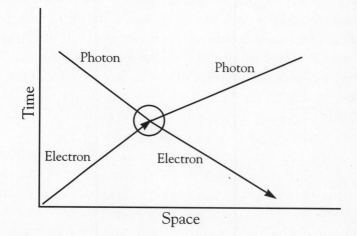

Did you spot the difference? One arrowhead has changed. In order to give an easy way of differentiating between particles and anti-particles, we have the arrowhead on particles pointing up and the arrowhead on anti-particles pointing down. If those arrowheads denote the direction of travel of the particles, the diagram now shows you have a particle (the electron on the left) that is moving forward in time and an anti-particle (the positron on the right) which is moving backwards.

This isn't sleight of hand. This is actually the way a physicist would draw it, because Feynman discovered all the way back in 1949 that, mathematically speaking, a positron moving forward in time is exactly the same thing as an electron moving backwards. Which brings us to the second small, important change. The anti-particle on the right is now labeled an electron just like the thing on the left.

Now you get a wholly different viewpoint on the subatomic event. Instead of a particle and an anti-particle colliding, what you have is an electron moving into the circled area, then disappearing in a flash of light (the two photons) as it abruptly turns to move backwards in time! Alternatively, and closer to the consensus, you are studying an electron which is annihilated to create three new particles—two photons and a new electron, but the new electron is also traveling back in time.

Here at last you have it. The sort of event shown in our little diagram actually happens. The interpretations we've applied since we changed the arrow are absolutely valid, but they both involve literal travel backwards through time, not as a permitted possibility, not as a theoretical probability, but as an actuality.

And if a subatomic particle can do it, so can you. All you need is a time machine.

CHAPTER TWENTY-ONE

By the 1970s, according to science writer Ed Regis, time travel had become "more or less an accepted possibility" among a more maverick element of North American physicists.[1] On the basis of four-dimensional Einsteinian space-time, they could not really see what there was to stop you. All you needed was a large enough mass, which was shown by the Relativity equations to warp the continuum.

One of the mavericks, the Austro-Canadian Hans Moravac, still held out some possibilities for Black Holes. Though he didn't believe you could survive a trip through one, he had an idea that you might just possibly be able to peer into them like a crystal ball to view the future. But it went to another physicist, Frank Tipler, to put the world's first time machine on the drawing board.

In the Seventies, Tipler was associated with the University of Maryland.[2] In 1974, he published his time travel ideas in *Physical Review* under the bewildering title "Rotating Cylinders and the Possibility of Global Causality Violation." It transpired that a global causality violation in this instance was as weird a piece of geometry as you're ever likely to come across: a path that winds through space and turns around in time.

This sort of thing is known among physicists as a pathology— something that doesn't behave the way they always assumed things should. Singularities are pathologies, of course, although pathologies aren't necessarily singularities. It's not commonly realized, but the General Theory of Relativity leaves a lot of room for pathologies and the awesome thing about this is that physicists today are coming to the conclusion they aren't just mathematical quirks.

Certainly, Tipler didn't believe his winding path pathology was a mathematical quirk. Nor did others thinking about time travel such as physicist Brandon Carter. They thought it might be possible to generate such a path by spinning a quantity of ultra-dense matter. But, why would they want to bother?

The answer to that lies in the predicted nature of the path. What you're talking about here is something that will take you through space-time, but includes a twist that will also take you back where you started, when you started. You could have a wonderful time for as long as you wanted, but to the outside world, you wouldn't have gone anywhere because you got back at the exact instant you left.

This sort of thing sounds like science fiction and bad science fiction at that. You're tempted to make jokes about not knowing whether you're coming or going. But physicists take it very seriously. They've even got a name for the path. They call it a closed timelike line.

The calculations show there are closed timelike lines associated with rotating Black Holes: you have to go through Black Holes twice to complete the loop. They are also associated with wormholes and here again it's a dual trip—you have to squeeze through a brace of wormholes on your closed timelike path to come out in the same universe you left, let alone the same place and the same time. Fairly obviously, Tipler's idea of generating such a path under (more or less) controlled conditions seems a lot safer than walking the natural paths created by Black Holes and wormholes.

So, how did Tipler propose it might be done? He said it all in a single sentence: "General Relativity suggests that if we construct a sufficiently large rotating cylinder, we create a time machine."[3]

Brandon Carter, speaking about a similar sort of set-up, said, "The central region [of the space-time warp] has the properties of a time machine. It is possible, starting from any point in the outer regions of the space, to travel to the interior, move backwards in time ... then return to the original position."[4]

It was that last bit that was getting the physicists so excited. Up to then, when you theorized about time travel, the really big problem was that everything you thought of seemed to be a one-way trip. If, somehow, you managed to get through a Black Hole or a wormhole in one piece, nobody would have given much for your chances of making the return trip accurately. You'd travel in time all right, forwards and back, but it was all out of control. The Black Hole might spit you out in Ancient Rome if you were very, very,

very lucky, but your luck would have to be astronomical to get you back within a hundred years of your own time. Our man in Mexico, if he really did pass through a wormhole, was fortunate that his displacement was along the spatial and not the temporal axis. At least there were ships to carrying him back to the Philippines. If he'd shifted in time, he'd have been stuck where he landed.

The theory behind the Tipler cylinder was straightforward enough. If it's big enough and dense enough and spinning fast enough, it warps space-time in a particular way. The term used to describe it is sinusoid, which sounds like an illness but is actually the name for anything that swings, or bends or otherwise fluctuates to return to its original state. The pendulum of my wife's grandfather clock is on a sinusoid path in space—it always returns to the point where it started, at least until I forget to wind the clock.

Tipler's sinusoid warp is not just in space, but in space-time. It distorts the fabric so that instead of following its old familiar path from past to future, time actually oscillates. It swings backwards and forwards like the pendulum of the grandfather clock. Catch it on one swing and you're moving forward in time. Catch it on another and you're traveling backwards. The oscillations form zones. If you're very careful, you might be able to fly into a backward-running time zone without getting yourself ripped to pieces by the forces of gravity.

Diagram F (below) is of a Tipler cylinder with its more important associated zones as shown in Fred Alan Wolf's *Parallel Universes*. It's not to scale and you're looking at it end-on.

The cylinder itself is the shaded circle in the middle. It's gigantic, it's dense and it's rotating, which is what creates the zones in the first place.

Immediately surrounding the cylinder is a twenty-kilometer wide zone where the fabric of space-time is grossly distorted. On the diagram, this is labeled the Deadly zone. There is no way you could exist in such a zone. In fact, most physicists are convinced you couldn't get into it in the first place—you would be repelled by the very nature of space-time at its outer boundary.

Surrounding the deadly zone is the really interesting one, the zone of time reversal. This is the area of space where the sinusoid

Diagram F: The Tipler Cylinder and the Zones

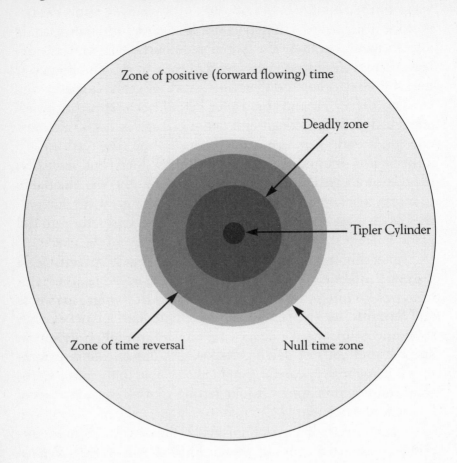

Zone of positive (forward flowing) time

Deadly zone

Tipler Cylinder

Zone of time reversal

Null time zone

oscillation generated by the spinning cylinder means that time runs backwards. Get yourself into that zone and you're a time traveler.

The time travel zone is surrounded by a null time zone, representing the interface between negative time to one side and positive time to the other. In the null time zone, time stands still. This zone is surrounded by a positive time zone—one, that is, where time runs in the familiar past-to-future direction.

That's the machine on the drawing board. Could one be constructed in the real world? The answer is yes, but not yet. Tipler was content to expound the theory of a time machine, but the imaginative Fred Alan Wolf has gone a step further to show how, at least potentially, one might really be built.

The greatest problem with the Tipler Cylinder is what to make it from. It's not enough to forge a giant cylinder in steel or extrude it in plastic. Using that sort of material, the thing would need to be so large it would fill the galaxy. What you want is some sort of super-dense material, the sort that has a huge mass, but takes up very little room. That sort of matter actually exists, at the very nucleus of atoms. It's the densest substance in the universe. If you could extract enough to fill a teaspoon, it would weigh more than one billion tons.

It should be obvious from this that you couldn't actually extract appreciable quantities of nucleus material in the laboratory even if you happened to discover the technique, but that doesn't matter. As Wolf points out, Nature has already done it for you. You could (theoretically) mine nucleus material on any neutron star.

Neutron stars, you will recall, are those stars which suffer gravitational collapse but do not go all the way to becoming a Black Hole. The electrons of their atoms instead of orbiting sedately as Rutherford envisaged are plunged into the nucleus where they fuse with protons to become neutrons (hence the name neutron star). The atoms themselves are fused together so that the whole star becomes one great atomic nucleus. Here, at last, is the ideal material to build your Tipler Cylinder.

Except that to build a cylinder of manageable proportions, you wouldn't just need material mined from a neutron star, you'd need the whole star. In fact, you'd actually need more than one. Wolf estimates that a working Tipler cylinder would have to be about 40 kilometers across and 4,000 kilometers long. Function determines this size. The whole design is a trade-off. You need something that generates a reverse time zone far enough away from its spinning surface so a human could enter the zone without being crushed by gravity. To do that, you need a very long cylinder.

To get yourself a 4,000 km long cylinder, you will need about a hundred neutron stars. This seems a lot, but while they have immense mass, neutron stars are (in stellar terms) very small.

Both the gravity generated by a hundred neutron stars and the length of the Tipler Cylinder they form clearly determine that your time machine is not going to be built on Earth. Four thousand kilometers is about the width of the United States, but even if you persuaded the Senate to permit it, the gravitational mass would destroy our planet. So, the Tipler Cylinder will have to be constructed somewhere in space, preferably an area of space where there is little or no natural gravitational interference. Wolf has the fancy that star wranglers, using unimaginably advanced technology, will herd the neutron stars together.

Tipler's plans call not only for a cylinder, but a spinning cylinder. Fortunately, most neutron stars are already spinning on their own axes. Wolf calculates that the cylinder will need a rotation of around 10,000 revolutions per second, which, fortunately, falls within the range of the typical neutron star. By synchronizing the 10,000 revolution spins of a hundred neutron stars herded together in a line, you have a cylinder which, at its surface, is spinning at about three quarters the speed of light. This does very nicely to produce the zones we've been discussing at a distance far enough from the cylinder for us to be able to use them.

Once your cylinder is in place and spinning, the time machine is ready to use. To do so, have your ship's computer plot a course that lets you approach the cylinder end on. If you approach at right angles—or, indeed, any oblique angle—to the axis of spin you will not be able to reach the inner zone you need, but since the zones are rings, not spheres, you can come at them sideways.

Because of particle interactions, the zones are quite visible. For example, the deadly zone around the cylinder glows rather prettily as matter-antimatter annihilations generate violet photons. Your space-time ship would aim for the second zone, the time travel zone, on a trajectory parallel to the axis of the cylinder. When it enters the zone, you are no longer flying through space. You have switched to the fourth dimensional axis and are flying through time.

Given the technology to harness neutron stars, a time machine based on the plans for a Tipler Cylinder is perfectly feasible. We are nowhere close to that technology today, but it would be nonsense to insist we could never produce it in the future. So, is some version of the cylinder the likely means by which the South African spheres were transported to Precambrian Earth? Did the "tourists" who lost their lives in the Pliocene, the Miocene, the Oligocene, the Carboniferous, slip through our reverse time zone?

There is one aspect of this type of travel we have not yet mentioned that may help us towards an answer.

Although calculations show a Tipler Cylinder could generate usable zones, they would still place considerable gravitational strain on the time traveler. In order to minimize the effect (and in particular the gravitational differential between top and bottom) Wolf suggests the only logical shape for a timeship would be a flattened disc—what one might call a flying saucer.

Endnotes

1. In *Great Mambo Chicken and the Transhuman Condition*.
2. As of 1994, he was Professor of Physics and Mathematics at Tulane University in New Orleans.
3. In *Great Mambo Chicken and the Transhuman Condition*.
4. Ibid.

CHAPTER TWENTY-TWO

Accounts of flying saucers usually begin with the experience of Kenneth Arnold in 1947. Arnold, a civilian pilot, was flying his own single-engined plane over Mount Rainier (Washington State) on a search mission for a crashed transport when he saw nine disc-shaped objects flying by in two parallel lines. Triangulation of their speed gave an approximate figure of 1,600 mph, well beyond the capabilities of any aircraft of the day. When Arnold reported the sighting later, he described the objects as moving "like a saucer would if you skipped it across the water."[1] The term stuck. Flying saucers were born.

Arnold did not, so far as I'm aware, suggest the saucers were alien spacecraft, but others very quickly did. Only five years later came the first claim that a flying saucer had landed.

The man who made it was an American named George Adamski. In a book he later co-authored,[2] he described how the craft came down some ten miles from California's Desert Center on the afternoon of November 20, 1952. An extraordinarily handsome, long-haired man in a chocolate brown ski-suit climbed out. Adamski questioned him using a mixture of sign language and "telepathy" (he visualized what he wanted to know). The man indicated that he came from the planet Venus and was concerned about atomic test explosions on Earth which were affecting the environment of space. After some further "conversation" (during which the alien acknowledged belief in God) they strolled together to the spaceship, and the Venusian took off.

The information Adamski obtained during this experience is, of course, nonsense. We now know conditions on the planet Venus preclude life. (The surface temperature is hot enough to melt lead.) Even in Adamski's day, there were questions asked about how an alien managed to survive in Earth's atmosphere without a pressure suit or helmet. Desmond Leslie, who co-authored Adamski's book, was forced to conclude things were not exactly as they seemed. He told me some years later he thought Adamski's visitor had actually come from the astral plane of Venus. Others were far less sympathetic. Many concluded Adamski was suffering from hallucinations or simply lying. These conclusions were reinforced by the publication of a second book in which Adamski claimed he had been taken on a trip in a flying saucer which circled the moon before dropping him home again.

Tempting though the lunacy explanation might be, there are problems with it. Almost all Adamski's critics ignore the fact that he was not alone when he first met his "Venusian." There were six others with him, all of whom were prepared to sign affidavits swearing they had also seen the craft and its pilot. Also ignored is that fact that following his lunar trip, Adamski noted some utterly unexpected peculiarities about space flight—including an odd optical illusion on the moon's surface—that were subsequently confirmed by the American space program.

None of this proves Adamski was not a crank, but it may support the possibility of an alternative explanation. If the saucer shape is the most logical design for a timeship—a spacecraft which squeezes through the warp field generated by a Tipler Cylinder—then perhaps the creature Adamski met was exactly what he seemed: a long-haired man in a chocolate ski-suit. He was just as human as Adamski himself, but originated in a distant future. If this theory is correct, why did he claim to come from Venus and express concern about atomic tests? There are two possibilities. One is that an overawed Adamski utterly misunderstood the sign language and the "telepathic" messages. When asked his origins, the man pointed to the sky and made two circuits with his finger. Adamski interpreted this as indicating a planet in the second orbit around the sun—i.e. Venus. We might equally well see it as indicating two passes around a Tipler Cylinder established somewhere in the depths of space. The other, even simpler possibility, is that Adamski and his friends weren't lying, but the "Venusian" was. He spun a fantastic yarn to hide his real origins.

It is probably true to say Adamski's experience was considered too outrageous for any serious investigation by the authorities, but Arnold's original report was not. Arnold was a respected businessman and experienced pilot and a year after his Mount Rainier sightings, the United States Air Force created Project Sign to investigate these and other reports which were by now beginning to flood in. Project Sign metamorphosed into Project Grudge, then into Project Blue Book.

The purpose of Project Blue Book was the evaluation of UFO sightings to determine whether they represented a threat to the United States from any foreign power, or from outer space. Over a period of eighteen years, it accumulated 12,600 reports. Of these, 11,899 were subsequently explained (critics of the Project would say "explained away"), leaving 701 still a mystery. In 1966, the U.S. Air Force sponsored an additional independent investigation headed by the physicist Dr. Edward Condon, who was a former head of the American Association for the Advancement of Science. Over the next two years, fifty-nine cases were investigated of which twenty-three remained unexplained. Rather surprisingly under the circumstances, Dr. Condon issued a final report in 1969 which concluded UFO study had added nothing to scientific knowledge and absolutely dismissed the possibility that the saucers were evidential of extraterrestrial life. The Air Force apparently agreed and ceased all official investigation of UFOs from that date.[2]

Official dismissal has done nothing to stem the flood of sightings, however. Since 1947, UFOs have appeared in nearly every country of the globe. Oddly enough, the number of sightings does not remain static from year to year, but shows a pattern of occasional sudden peaks. For example, UFO peaks occurred in France and Italy in 1954, in New Guinea in 1958, and in the USSR in 1967. In the United States, peaks occurred in 1947, 1952, 1957, 1965–67, and 1973. UFO researchers have been unable to predict or explain these peaks. Attempts to link them to media publicity, hysterical contagion, or societal stress have been unsuccessful.

The number of UFO sightings is far higher than most people imagine. In 1973 a Gallup poll indicated that eleven percent of the adult population in the United States had seen what they thought was a UFO. More than 50,000 worldwide sighting reports have been computerized—a figure generally accepted to represent the very small tip of a very large iceberg. A study of these reports suggests that UFO sightings are random, and no pattern of

UFO witnesses has been found. Witnesses cut across economic, class, racial, and educational lines and include at least one American President.[4] A greater percentage of reports, however, have come from people living in rural areas than from those living in urban areas. The reasons for this disparity are unknown, although it may simply be that country-dwellers get a better view of the night sky than their city cousins.

The majority of reports are of objects seen at great distance, but close observations also exist. Some of the most intriguing of them are objects seen on or near the ground. Often, the person claims that the object left a residue or mark. Sometimes, the object is claimed to have had a physical effect on an electrical or mechanical device, causing television interference or automobile engines to stall. Approximately ninety percent of raw UFO reports are interpreted as misperceptions of conventional objects, hoaxes, or hallucinations. The remaining ten percent constitute the UFO enigma.

A fascinating, if disturbing, development within the enigma in recent years has been the number of reports claiming abduction, sexual abuse, rape, and even impregnation carried out by extraterrestrial UFOnauts on terrestrial women and, in the first three instances, men. Fairly typical is the case of Antonio Villas Boas, a twenty-three-year-old Brazilian farmer who was abducted in October 1957. While on board the craft, he was subjected to blood tests before a beautiful naked woman entered the room and seduced him. When she left she indicated she was (or hoped to be) pregnant.

Accounts of such abductions, often extracted under hypnosis from amnesiac patients, ignore two very basic questions. The first is why the product of an alien evolution should show any more sexual interest in an Earth woman than, for example, an alligator. The second, rather more telling, is the unlikelihood of inter-species breeding. A lion might, under rare circumstances, mate with a tiger to produce a tigon, but it cannot, under any circumstances, reproduce with a wolf, an elephant, or a snake. The genetic incompatibility is simply too extreme, but this degree of incompatibility is insignificant compared with the genetic incompatibility of a wholly alien species—even assuming that species reproduced sexually in the first place.

Yet, the sheer volume of abduction reports—which now run into tens of thousands worldwide and increasing—make them a phenomenon worthy of study in their own right. Are we dealing with mass sexual hysteria? The outward projection of repressed emotions? Hallucination generated by frustration?

It is worth pointing out that, contrary to the more dismissive critics, flying saucers have a physical reality. They show up on radar screens and have been successfully photographed many times over. Even allowing for ninety percent mistaken identity, there is no doubt that something is up there and the numbers of reports now in place indicate quite a heavy volume of traffic. In such circumstances, it may be unwise to dismiss every abduction case as hallucination.

If, however, it is unlikely that aliens would be interested in, or even equipped for, rape, the same cannot be said for humanity. Sexual violence, fascination, and experimentation have been a central feature of human activity from the depths of prehistory and will certainly continue to be a central feature of human activity for centuries to come. Here, too, as in Adamski's all-too-human "Venusian," we have an indication that flying saucers may not be craft from an alien planet, but craft from a distant future of our own.

Short of capturing a pilot, I can see no way of proving this thesis. If we accept it for the moment as a working hypothesis, we generate a second series of evidence to complement the anomalous finds of archaeology. For while many surveys of saucers begin with the Arnold sighting, the saucers themselves go back a much longer time.

Unlike anomalous finds, which are far easier to spot in prehistory than modern times, most saucer sightings are, almost by definition, an historical phenomenon. All the same, several rock carvings in the Hunan province of China have been taken to represent UFOs. If this interpretation is correct, the timeships must have been studying Neanderthal humanity, not *Homo sapiens*. The carvings have been dated as 47,000 years old.

An Egyptian text, dating to the reign of Thutmose III (1504-1450 B.C.) describes how:

"In the year 22 of the third month of winter, sixth hour of the day ... the scribes of the House of Life found it was a circle of fire that was coming in the sky .... Now after some days had passed, these things became more numerous in the skies than ever. They shone more in the sky than the brightness of the sun .... The army of the Pharaoh looked on with him in their midst .... Thereupon these fire circles ascended higher in the sky towards the south ... And what happened was ordered by the Pharaoh to be written in the annals of the House of Life ... so that it be remembered forever."[5]

Thutmose III was not a fanciful monarch. He is generally looked on as the greatest of Egypt's warrior kings. He expanded and consolidated Egyptian control over an empire of unprecedented extent in western Asia and Africa. Between 1482 and 1462 B.C., he personally led many victorious campaigns in Syria, Palestine, and Phoenicia. In a battle on the east bank of the Euphrates, he defeated the powerful kingdom of Mitanni, his chief rival for control of the Near East. Meanwhile, his armies in Nubia pushed beyond the Nile's fourth cataract. Thutmose set up an efficient administration in the conquered territories, in which vassal kings and chiefs were forced to pay heavy tribute to Egypt. Hardly the career of someone prone to day-dreaming.

Saucers were also sighted in Ancient Rome. Julius Obsequens records a "round shield" seen in the sky about 180 miles east of Rome in 216 B.C., a "round or circular shield" which flew west to east across the sky over Tarquinia in 99 B.C. and something similar, but more fiery, which landed, then took off again in the territory of Spoletium in 90 B.C.

A sixteenth-century author, Professor Conrad Wolffhart, records UFO formations at the time of Emperor Theodosius in A.D. 393. There are reports of saucers over France in A.D. 1034, over Japan in 1180 (described, curiously enough, as a flying 'earthenware vessel') and over England in the twelfth century. A contemporary description of this last sighting reads:

"At Byland or Begeland Abbey in the North Yorkshire Riding, while the abbot and monks were in the refectorium, a discus flew over the abbey and caused the utmost terror."[6]

It would be tortuous to attempt to chronicle each UFO sighting throughout history. It may, perhaps, be enough to say that every single century back to ancient times has had its reports of UFO visitations. If the saucers really are timeships, it is clear that future historians have been having a field day.

Endnotes

1. From *Grolier Electronic Encyclopedia*. Entry under "Unidentified Flying Objects."

2. *Flying Saucers Have Landed* by Desmond Leslie and George Adamski, Neville Spearman, London, 1970.

3. My many friends who accept the reality of flying saucers rush to underline that word *official*. They claim, with what justification I am unqualified to judge, that the authorities in virtually every country on earth have secret projects running, and that public statements to the contrary are part of a worldwide cover-up to avoid panic about what is actually a very mysterious and frightening situation.

4. Jimmy Carter, who filed an official UFO report while he was Governor of Georgia. When political opponents used this to try to prove he was a crank during his election campaign, Carter played down his experience with the humorous suggestion that it might have been "a star beckoning him towards the White House."

5. Quoted in *Mysteries of the Unexplained*, Carroll C. Calkins (ed.) Reader's Digest Books, London, 1982.

6. Quoted from *William of Newburg's Chronicle*.

CHAPTER TWENTY-THREE

The theory that our descendants may one day construct a Tipler Cylinder has an interesting implication. If the time-field generated by the cylinder exists in the future and saucer-like craft use it to access our own time, it follows logically that the field must also exist now. If it didn't, no timeship could return home. This is an exciting thought. It means that somewhere beyond the orbit of Pluto lies a timegate that you and I could actually use to visit the past or the future. Unfortunately, in practical terms, this knowledge is useless to us. Current technology might, with a massive investment, carry us to Mars. We have nothing that would carry us safely beyond Pluto. So, short of following George Adamski's example and hitching a lift on a passing flying saucer, travel through time is debarred for us.

Or is it?

We have now reached a critical juncture in our study, and like many critical junctures, this one requires a real effort of understanding. There have been developments in physics that are so weird, so contrary to our normal world view that it is difficult to take them seriously—or at least difficult to believe they could have any personal relevance to you or me. If you can follow the logic and accept the implications, I think I may be able to promise you a quite extraordinary experience.

The critical juncture first manifested in 1935 when Albert Einstein, ably abetted by his old friends Nathan Rosen and Boris Podolsky, managed to shoot himself in the foot. Einstein, you will recall, was the man who based his whole world view on a single insight—you can't push things faster than the speed of light. If he knew anything with absolute certainty, he knew that.

In 1935, he wasn't concerned with the speed of light—that had long been settled. He was concerned with something called the Copenhagen Interpretation. The Copenhagen Interpretation was a consensus belief among a large group of respected physicists that quantum physics represented a complete explanation of the universe we live in. Einstein didn't agree. Like everyone else in physics, he thought it provided the very best current explanation,[1] but not a complete explanation. What really troubled him was the What You See Is What You Get aspect of quantum physics. The whole of quantum theory tells you that you can't separate reality from your observation of reality. This is a baby step away from the sort of mystical and occult ideas that you actually create reality by the action of your mind. Einstein didn't like it.

In collaboration with Podolsky and Rosen, who didn't like it either, he published a paper called *Can Quantum-Mechanical Description of Reality be Considered Complete?* In it, they described an experiment which they figured proved it couldn't be. The experiment, as explained by physicist David Bohm, was this:

You start with a twin-particle system with zero spin. The twin particle system is a thing complete in itself, not just a convenient marriage of two separate particles. Each particle in the system has its own spin, but the reason the system as a whole has no spin is that the spins of the two particles happen to be equal and opposite—in other words they cancel each other out.

It's possible to separate the particles of such a system without influencing the spin factor at all. You could, for example, do it electrically. You can also influence the spin of each individual particle. All you need do here is push it through a magnetic field. But if you do this and change the spin of one of the particles, the spin of the twin particle also changes so the overall system remains at zero spin.

The question is, now that you've separated out the two particles, how does the second particle know it has to change when you've pushed the first particle through a magnetic field. The second particle doesn't go through a magnetic field. You don't do anything to it at all, but it still changes. How?

Einstein et al dumped that one in the laps of the Copenhagen physicists saying, in effect: If quantum mechanics is so damn smart, how come it can't explain those apples? Or, in more dignified terms: Quantum mechanics cannot be a complete theory since it does not describe certain aspects of reality—like the linkage between the two particles of a twin particle system—which we know to be present even though we cannot directly observe it.

That was where Einstein shot himself in the foot—a shot which, incidentally, still reverberates through the world of nuclear physics, because the Copenhagen physicists didn't abandon their idea that quantum mechanics was a complete theory. Instead, they looked at the Einstein-Podolsky-Rosen experiment and decided it demonstrated a hitherto unsuspected connection between the two particles. They even, rather cheekily in the circumstances, called it the EPR (Einstein-Podolsky-Rosen) Effect.

The sting in the tail of the EPR Effect is that when you change the spin of one particle, the spin of the other changes instantaneously. This happens however far you separate them. For the second particle to change at all, there must be an information exchange between them. But the EPR Effect means the information is being carried by something that moves faster than the speed of light.

Einstein, who believed in the speed of light the way some people believe in God, could not accept this at all. He wrote in his autobiography:

> On one supposition we should, in my opinion, absolutely hold fast: the real factual situation of the system S2 [the particle you don't touch] is independent of what is done with the system S1 [the particle you do] which is spatially separated from the former.[2]

By now, the young Turk who had so revolutionized physics had become the established conservative who wished, like so many of us, to cling to old certainties. Had he retained his former flexibility, he might have realized, as he once had, that the result of experiment is the only place to stand. Twisting one particle influences the other: you can't get away from that. If it means super light speed communication, you live with it and try to explain it.

By the time of Einstein's death in 1955, there were already serious problems arising around the speed of light. Scientists had discovered that far from being an absolute, it actually varied. Hard though it is to believe, light traveled slower in 1930 than it did after World War II. The variation got so bad that physicists had to fix the speed by definition in 1972.

Even this did nothing to explain the EPR Effect. Nor did terms like telepathy, which were bandied about disparagingly among the opposing factions. All the old explanations ran into difficulties—except one. Physicists began to postulate a basic unity of phenomena, the sort of wholeness, the sort of oneness that mystics have claimed for centuries to be the ultimate reality. The big difference between the mystics and the physicists is that the mystics speak about the unity of the universe. The physicists are talking about a unity of space-time.

This is where physics goes out of sight. Remember we are now talking about a reality where space and time are rolled together in one great fabric. A reality where matter distorts the fabric and maybe (if Einstein's suspicions were correct) where matter actually is the distortion of the fabric. A reality where things only make sense if you have more than one universe and where the multitude of universes interact all the time. And now the physicists are telling you everything, but everything in that vast, unimaginable reality is a unity. It knows what happens to its bits in the same way you know where to scratch when you have an itch, but it doesn't just know in space—it also knows in time. Since you are part of that whole, that essential unity, you also know in time as well.

Fred Wolf explains using the example of a single light particle. This photon, he asks us to consider, was emitted a minute or two after the multiverse came into being at the Big Bang about 15 billion years ago. It's been traveling towards you here on Earth ever since. You remember, of course, that light doesn't go straight—it's bent by gravity. So, when our photon passed high gravity sources, like galaxies or Black Holes, it's deflected. Which way is it deflected? It's impossible to say for sure: there are no certainties in particle physics, only probabilities. This means that the photon might take any one of several different routes to reach you, but for the sake of simplicity, let's suppose there are really only two.

If you sit quietly waiting for the photon to arrive and only see it when it does arrive,[3] the particle travels along both paths. I know this is impossible, but we're speaking in quantum terms. In quantum terms, the two probability universes open to the particle are fused together until an observation is made. So, since you haven't bothered to make an observation, the quantum reality is that the particle behaved like a wave and not a little cannon ball. The wave moved along both paths.

If you decide you want to know which route the photon took, you can set up video cameras at a convenient point on both routes and watch out for it. This creates an entirely different quantum situation. It means that the particle must behave like a little cannon ball and go down one path or the other. So, as soon as you decide to observe the particle, it only moves along one path.

If you've followed this so far, you're ready for the big one.

The particle started moving along one path or two 15 billion years ago, but you only decided whether or not to watch out for it just last week. So, a decision you made last week influenced a situation 15 billion years ago. Which means your decision, in the present, can influence the past. It also suggests that your decisions, in the future, can influence your present. This is the exact reverse of the way we always thought time worked. We always thought that actions and decisions today created our future. Now it looks like actions and decisions today create our past. In terms of causality, we're living backwards. Remember that notion of starting your life in a grave and ending it siphoned off by your dad? Maybe it's not so crazy after all.

You could not possibly be expected to take something like this on trust, even though the hypothetical situation with the photon is in exact accord with the laws of quantum mechanics. The really bad news is that it has been verified experimentally. This was done in 1985 in Maryland, U.S.A. by three physicists: Carroll Alley, Oleg Jakubowicz and William Wickes. They fired a single photon through an apparatus made from mirrors. It set up in miniature exactly the situation I've just described to you. Insert one particular mirror and the photon passed through two channels simultaneously. Take it out and the photon passed through one or the other. But the physicists only took their decision about the mirror after the photon had entered the system. Their present decision influenced the past behavior of the photon.

There is one way out of this with your sanity intact. You can convince yourself that whatever happens to photons has nothing to do with you. After all, most of the worst excesses of the subatomic world have stayed in the subatomic world. But before you get too comfortable, let me introduce you to a physicist called J. S. Bell.

In 1964, Bell published something that's now known as Bell's Theorem. The theorem is a purely mathematical construction based on a study of the EPR Effect. It was experimentally tested by John Clauser and Stuart Freedman at the Lawrence Berkeley Laboratories in 1972 and found to work. The bottom line of Bell's Theorem is that quantum effects expressed in the subatomic world of particles reach into the macroscopic world of baseball games and double-decker buses. You can no longer trust your common sense. You can no longer be quite sure of the obvious. You can no longer assume you live your life forwards, traveling away from a past that's lost and gone towards a future that you create as you go along. Bell's Theorem has ended all that and the world can never be the same again.

But it's not all bad news. It may actually allow you—yes you—to time travel.

Endnotes

1. It still does.

2. Quoted by Gary Zukav in *The Dancing Wu Li Masters*.

3. You actually could see it. When your eye adapts fully to darkness, it can sense a single photon.

CHAPTER TWENTY-FOUR

One of the great mysteries of modern physics is where and how the human mind fits in. We've known for a long time that it definitely does fit in. Heisenberg's Uncertainty Principle, a pillar of the new physics, is based on the fact that you can't measure both the speed and the location of a subatomic particle. You can measure the speed or you can measure the location, but it's not possible to measure both. Physicists don't know why this is, but they do know what brings the situation about: the act of observation. Once you look at one aspect of the situation (say the particle's location), you automatically and absolutely shut down any possibility of looking at the other. Some experts try to fuzz the picture by insisting that the act of observation can be made by a camera or some other instrument, but all this does is push the problem back a step. Realistically, nothing happens until you, or a scientist or some intelligence somewhere examines the picture in the camera. There is no getting away from it. The human mind is not just part of the universe, it actually influences the universe continually at a very profound level.

A great many physicists have a great many theories about how far the influence extends. Some of them would make your hair curl. Fred Hoyle, for example, had the idea that by sliding through parallel universes you might wake up each morning beside a different spouse. But since your memory traces would be consistent only with the universe you happened to be in, you wouldn't realize anything had changed. Professor Hoyle put that one forward in a novel, so maybe he didn't take it too seriously, but the theory is actually consistent with the findings of quantum mechanics. He does take seriously the idea that many parallel universes are constructed by overlays from the future. Hugh Everett, the physicist who came up with parallel universe theory in the first place, thinks memory may be a selection of images stored in a number of parallel universes. This would make what we think of as our single, consistent past an unsuspected montage from a host of different sources.

In 1969, two physicists—Leon Cooper and Deborah Van Vechten—announced their theory that if a mind was simple enough, it might be able to experience two parallel realities at the same time. They believed, however, that minds as complex as our own would have problems doing so.

This is an extraordinarily interesting statement. But to understand why, we have to look beyond physics itself. It has frequently been remarked—by Gary Zukav, Fritjof Capra, Deepak Chopra, and others—that there is a remarkable similarity between the findings of modern physics and certain mystical teachings. Zukav puts it this way:

> "Subatomic particles forever partake of this unceasing dance of annihilation and creation. In fact, subatomic particles are this unceasing dance of annihilation and creation. This twentieth-century discovery ... is not a new concept. In fact, it is very similar to the way that much of the earth's population, including the Hindus and the Buddhists, view their reality."

Hindu mythology is virtually a large-scale projection ... of microscopic scientific discoveries. Hindu deities such as Shiva and Vishnu continually dance the creation and destruction of universes while the Buddhist image of the wheel of life symbolizes the unending process of birth, death and rebirth which is part of a world of form, which is emptiness, which is form.[1]

The oriental faiths which propound these doctrines are not revealed religions like Judaism, Christianity, and Islam. They are mystically based. That is to say, they are based on the interpretation of a peculiar psychological state experienced by their founders and/or practitioners. This state, it is believed, gives an individual direct access to the fundamental nature of reality. The agreement between the doctrines of mysticism and the findings of quantum physics suggests that the mystic claims are accurate—mystical insight really is a direct perception of reality. Zukav again:

"There is speculation, and some evidence, that consciousness, at the most fundamental level, is a quantum
process... If this is so, then it is conceivable that by ex-
panding our awareness to include functions which normally lie beyond its parameters ... we can become aware of
(experience) these processes themselves."[2]

The University of London physicist David Bohm goes even
further. He theorizes that the universe is holographic in structure,
a projection from another level of reality which contains, in each
of its pieces, information about the whole. The same conclusion
was reached independently by the Stanford University neuro-
physiologist Karl Pribram. Their ideas received some degree of
experimental support in 1982 when a team led by Alain Aspect
of the Institute of Theoretical and Applied Optics in Paris discovered that separated particles influenced each other simultaneously when they were ten meters apart. The result makes a little
more sense in a holographic universe than it does in the more
conventional picture.

The holographic universe theory has been embraced enthusi-
astically by many physicists and psychologists because it provides
a welcome explanation for a whole range of anomalous phenomena. Dr Kenneth Ring, the University of Connecticut psychologist, used it to explain near-death experiences—the result, so he
argued in 1980, of consciousness shifting from one level of the
hologram to another. The ubiquitous Fred Alan Wolf told a meeting of the Association for the Study of Dreams in 1987 that the
new theory suggested lucid dreams might be visits to parallel realities. The Canadian physicist Dr F. David Peat saw meaningful
coincidences as flaws in the fabric of holographic reality.

What all the excitement came down to was the realization
that our thought processes are much more intimately connected
with the physical world than had hitherto been suspected—further scientific support for the mystic's claim that direct experience
of quantum processes is possible.

The royal road to mystical experience has always been yogic
practice. Yoga systems have appeared throughout the Far East,

notably in India and China, with similar methods achieving similar results. They have even appeared in Europe, usually masquerading as occult or magical techniques. The most fundamental technique of all, universally used in both East and West, is meditation. Here we return full circle to the theory of Leon Cooper and Deborah Van Vechten that a simple mind might be able to experience two parallel realities, for the entire practice of meditation, in every yogic system, is designed to still (i.e., simplify) the mind.

It is not generally realized that certain mystical systems—notably those in the West—postulate one or more parallel universes, but insist that these realities can be directly sensed by humanity. The means by which this may be done is the human imagination, a psychological function devalued by most of us, but held by mystical tradition to operate almost as an organ of sight. When you use imagination, according to this perspective, you are actually gazing into another world, a space-time continuum different from the physical reality around you, but just as objective, just as real. The fact that it does not always look like a parallel universe is explained by the bizarre nature of the continuum itself.

If you close your eyes and visualize a scarecrow, the result is entirely within your control. You can make the image move around at will. You can have it stand on its head, turn somersaults or talk. It is obviously something you created, not something you searched for and found in a parallel universe, but mystical doctrine insists the scarecrow actually existed, for a short time at least, elsewhere. It was created by the action of your mind on the tenuous, subtle matter of the parallel universe, which has extraordinary malleability. It can be molded and shaped with an ease unknown in the physical universe. It is, in other words, a world which gives form to thoughts. It is also a world which contains reflections from at least some of the series of parallel dimensions which lie, so to speak, beyond.

In the past, it has been all too easy to dismiss theories of this sort as so much mumbo jumbo. Their adherents claimed they were the result not of experiment, but of direct experience. The scientific assumption was that the so-called "experience" was no more than subjective psychological processes. It is now quite clear that this assumption is no longer safe. Physicists not only speculate that alternative realities may be experienced directly (as in Wolf's ideas about lucid dreaming), but quantum physics itself confirms the validity of much information obtained by purely mystical means.

If, however, the mystical theories are correct—if, that is, parallel realities can be experienced directly—then the possibility arises of experiential time travel. As we have seen, the findings of quantum physics suggest that some, at least, of the parallel universes are images of our historical past and distant future. Accessing those realities by means of the visual imagination would be time travel by any reasonable definition.

But, is there any real evidence such access may be possible?

Endnotes

1. Quoted from *The Dancing Wu Li Masters*.
2. Ibid.

CHAPTER TWENTY-FIVE

In April 1994, archaeologist Brian Slade published[1] a brief but startling article titled "An Archaeologist Confesses." What he confessed to was using dowsing to locate ancient remains.

Dowsing is the practice of using a forked stick to discover underground water, buried metal, or metal ores. It is an ancient divining technique that, although never scientifically explained or proven in a laboratory, has many adherents. Georgius Agricola, in his 1556 treatise on mining, *De re metallica*, mentions the use of a forked hazelwood stick to find silver ore in medieval German mines. Holding the two forks of a Y-shaped stick parallel with the ground, the dowser walks slowly over the search area. The stick dips toward the ground when it is over water or whatever is being sought. A dowser may also employ wood or iron rods, pendulums, or simply his or her own hands.

Theories of dowsing usually fall into two categories. The first suggests it is a purely psychological phenomenon. The dowser subconsciously picks up clues from his environment about the likely location of water or metal ore, and these are then translated into muscle tremors which influence the rod. The second theory is based on the idea that running water, and, presumably, metallic strata, generate a weak electrical field which is sensed by the dowser, again subconsciously, and indicated by the movement of the rod. Neither theory goes any way toward explaining how a dowser might locate ancient ruins which are neither running water nor metallic.

Yet Slade states categorically that in 1983 he carried out a detailed dowsing survey that convinced him much of the hilltop where he lived overlaid the remains of a seventh-to-ninth century Anglo-Saxon nunnery, an eleventh-to-sixteenth century Norman abbey, associated ancillary buildings, and parts of both the original and later cemetery areas. Sheppey Archaeological Society carried out excavations on the site some years later. Slade wrote:

"We unearthed seven seventh-ninth century Anglo-Saxon bronze dress pins, post-hole evidence for timber buildings of the same date, a 737–758 Saxon silver coin, four Henry III (1216–1272) 'long cross' silver pennies, samples of Anglo-Saxon glass, ten varieties of Roman pottery and as much Anglo-Saxon 'Ipswich ware' pottery as produced by all the excavations at Canterbury combined. This evidence was contemporary with the Anglo-Saxon Monasterium Sexburga complex founded ... circa 670 and with the Norman abbey built on the same site."

Slade also claimed that "directors of archaeological excavations occasionally recruit dowsers, but only after they are sworn to secrecy." Whatever about this, there is no doubt Slade is not the only archaeologist to have used dowsing in his profession. The late Tom Lethbridge, who built up a very solid reputation on the basis of his many finds, confessed on his retirement that he not only used dowsing, but also sometimes used what is called map dowsing. In this form of the practice, the dowser uses a rod or pendulum over a map of the site and makes his decisions accordingly. Whatever about the possibility of electrical fields or unconscious clues at the site itself, map dowsing would seem to be a total impossibility. Yet, it works.

One way to make sense of map dowsing—and, indeed, the sort of field dowsing Slade carried out—is to evoke the quantum concept of direct involvement by the human mind in the universe as a whole: in this instance, the specific involvement of the human mind in what we think of as the past. If current quantum pictures of a multiverse are correct, this actually means that the unconscious minds of dowsers are attuned in some instances to a parallel universe. In the case of Slade, this universe was a mirror of the past that interested him.

There seems to be little doubt that the unconscious mind can interact with the past in a way consistent with both mystical doctrine and quantum predictions. One classical case occurred in 1907 when the architect Frederick Bligh Bond was put in charge of excavating the ruins of Glastonbury Abbey. Bond had an interest in spiritualism and experimented with automatic writing, a process then believed to establish communication with the dead. During his experiments, Bond made contact with Gulielmus Monachus, William the Monk, who gave him detailed information about the Abbey in its heyday.

Today, automatic writing is generally considered to be a manifestation of the individual's unconscious mind. If so, Bligh Bond's unconscious was certainly reaching into other dimensions of reality, for the information he extracted enabled him to locate two hitherto lost chapels and eventually draw up a wholly accurate ground plan of the original Abbey.[2]

This same mental contact with the past is evident in the process of psychometry, but with the important difference that here the involvement is conscious. As used by psychologists, the term psychometry refers to the measurement of certain psychological phenomena. As used in psychical research, it refers to what might be called object reading—discerning the history of a particular object while in physical contact with it—and it is in this sense that the term is used here.

Psychometry works. Colin Wilson reports on an experiment carried out by the Metaphysic Institute in Paris in 1921 during which the painter and novelist Pascal Forthuny attempted to psychometrize a letter:

> "He began to improvise jokingly. 'Ah yes, I see a crime ... a murder...' When he had finished, Dr. [Gustav] Geley[3] said, 'That letter was from Henri Landru.' Landru was at the time on trial for the murder of eleven women—crimes for which he was guillotined in the following year.
> ...Geley's wife picked up a fan from the table. 'Let's see if that was just luck. Try this.'
> Still light hearted, Forthuny ran his fingers over the fan in a professional manner and looked solemnly into space. 'I have the impression of being suffocated. And I hear a name being called: Elisa!'
> Madame Geley looked at him in stupefaction. The fan had belonged to an old lady who had died seven years earlier from congestion of the lungs. The companion of her last days had been called Elisa.

... Madame Geley insisted on another experiment. She handed him an officer's cane. This time Forthuny looked serious as he let his fingers stray over it. He began to describe army maneuvers, somewhere in the Orient. He spoke of the young French officer who had owned the cane, of his return to France by sea, and of how the ship was torpedoed. He went on to say that the officer was rescued, but developed an illness and died two years later. Madame Geley verified that he was right in every particular.[4]

A more controlled example of the same talent arose during a course on the paranormal run by Professor Arthur Ellison at Loughborough University in 1992. Mrs. Jenny Bright gave a demonstration in which she held a number of objects in her left hand for a few minutes and made a total of 160 statements about their history. Of these, 125 were subsequently confirmed accurate. Here is an example of the quantum effect in action—a direct involvement by Mrs. Bright's mind in the past of the object she held.

Psychometry is a skill that involves the use of the visual imagination and can be taught to a surprisingly large number of people as we shall see presently. What differentiates between skilled and poor practitioners is the ability to ignore any personal associations they may have with the object and to describe clearly what they are seeing in the mind's eye.

Several other so-called "psychic talents" work in much the same way. Crystal gazing is one of many forms of divination in which the visible paraphernalia is no more than a stimulus to or focus of the psychic's imagination. As often as not, the information obtained by such methods refers to the past.

It appears then that the key to direct quantum experience of other realities, including time, is a particular use of the visual imagination. While this sounds straightforward, it is far from easy. The problem is that the imagination, as well as being a vehicle for what we might call quantum sight, is also continuously influenced by subjective factors—wish fulfillment, projections, daydreaming, etc. This is why the phenomenon of quantum sight is rare. Most of those who try to practice it distort their perceptions to such a degree that they become almost meaningless.

There are, however, various techniques to overcome—or at least reduce—this failing. The most successful of them have been combined into a two-day experimental program specially created for this book and tested successfully by groups in Britain and Ireland. The program is based on the statistical fact that a large percentage of the population can be taught in a very short time to psychometrize objects successfully, but it introduces a novel consensus check on the process which not only makes for more accurate reading, but creates a vivid inner experience which most people find extremely enjoyable.

The program is designed to permit you to conduct your own experiments with the direct perception of quantum reality. Specifically, it allows you to investigate the possibility of group time travel.

Endnotes

1. In *Fortean Times*, London, issue 74. April/May 1994.

2. When the Church authorities discovered how he had obtained the information, they fired him.

3. A leading French psychical researcher.

4. In *The Supernatural*, Robinson Publishing, London, 1991.

Part III

THE PROGRAM

CHAPTER TWENTY-SIX

The program is broken down into two parts—preparatory training and the actual experiment. To carry it through, you will need to gather a small group. The test groups varied in size between ten and twenty-five members, but it should be possible to function successfully with as few as five. The real prerequisite is dedication—while the experiment itself is usually very enjoyable, the preparation for it is fairly onerous.

Since the program is psychometry-based, you will need an object or an artifact from the time period your group wishes to investigate. This could be anything from a prehistoric arrowhead to a Medieval codpiece. If possible, the object should be something that has not been handled frequently in recent times. Each member of the group should also equip him/herself with a quartz crystal point, which will be used in a preliminary visualization focus practice and with a pair of wire coat hangers of the type used to return dry cleaning—the purpose of these will become clear shortly. You will also need at least one set of wire cutters or pliers.

Apart from this, all you need for the program is a room to carry out the experiment and a candle or night light which acts as a visual focus. A cassette tape recorder is an optional, but useful, additional piece of equipment.

Preliminary Training Technique 1

The training begins with a technique developed by psychologists to stimulate vivid dreaming. While vivid dreams certainly do sometimes result from its use, experience shows that it also has the effect of removing, at least temporarily, emotional encumbrances which might interfere with the final experiment.

For this technique it is necessary to break the working group into pairs. The process works best if paired couples do not know one another very well (if at all), although arranging pairs of strangers will not always be possible. Arbitrarily designate one member of each pair Member A, the second member becoming Member B.

Member A begins the process by selecting a room in his or her home or office that he or she is going to clean. This may be a living room, bedroom, dining room, bathroom or even garden shed. The vital thing is that it must be an actual room, existing in physical reality.

It is quite important that the individual follow his or her intuition in making the choice. Flexibility is important. For example, one participant in a seminar where the technique was used had only the week before moved house and wondered if he should clean a room in his old home rather than in the new bungalow which was not yet even fully furnished. Obviously, in a case like this it would be best to use a room from the old home. The only wholly inflexible rule is that the room must actually exist.

Have Member A decide what equipment he or she will have. Everything is readily available—buckets, sprays, detergents, soap, step ladders, and so on. Once these preliminary decisions have been made, Member A then begins to visualize cleaning the chosen room and tells Member B, in detail, exactly how this is being done.

The room should be cleaned in the following sequence:

- Start with the ceiling and clean it, then go down the walls.
- As you reach pictures, bookcases, etc., clean them and move them so you can clean behind them.
- Clean individual items such as books, ornaments as you come to them.
- If necessary, move furniture into the center of the room.
- When ceiling, walls, furnishings, and ornaments have all been cleaned, clean the carpet then lift the carpet and clean the floor underneath.

As you clean, decide what items you are going to keep and what you are going to throw out.

During the cleaning, store items you are going to throw away just outside the door. Small items go in a packing case, larger items can just be piled up in a heap. When completely finished, double-check on what you want to throw out and what you want to keep, making any necessary adjustments. Once you have finalized what you want rid of, go outside and either burn the lot in an imaginary bonfire, or dump it in an imaginary lake.

Throughout the entire process, it is important to have Member A describe what is going on in the greatest possible detail, right down to mentioning the color of ornaments, the titles of books, what scenes are shown in pictures, and so on.

When Member A has completely finished, there is a turn-around and Member B begins the process, describing in detail what is happening to Member A.

The exercise is complete when both members of each time have finished their processes.

This exercise should be followed by two others, both designed to deal in different ways with individual emotional problems which tend to interfere with the visualization process. The first of these is the Tower Exercise.

Preliminary Training Technique 2

The first step in the exercise is to have individual group members list up to seven of their current problems, numbering each one. When the members have done so, have them relax and imagine they face a door. When they feel ready, they should open the door and, in their imagination, pass through it. Tell them that once through, they stand outside a tall stone tower with a single entrance door of iron-studded oak standing slightly ajar.

Ask them to enter the tower in their imagination. When they do so, tell them that they find themselves in a large, single central room with one other door leading out of it and a stone spiral staircase winding around the outside. Inside this chamber, a huge log fire is burning, yet the chamber feels very cold. If they look upwards, they can see the reason for this—there are windows set at intervals along the whole height of the tower and each of them is open.

Have them climb the spiral staircase all the way to the top of the tower. Describe how their footsteps echo on the stone. As they go up, they will note there are a total of seven windows.

When they reach the end of the staircase, have them look through the top window and tell them there they will see a scene which symbolizes their first numbered problem. Allow them to look at this scene for a moment, then have them close the window. Explain this is not to deny the problem, not to ignore the problem, not to turn away from the problem, not even to solve the problem, but to stop them from losing energy to the problem.

When the window is closed, tell them to note that the problem transforms into something less threatening. Have them come down the stairs, repeating the process at each window and closing the windows one by one. Back in the central room, they should note that the atmosphere feels warmer because the windows are now shut. The question now arises: who opened the windows in the first place?

The answer you give them is that the windows were opened by their Saboteur. Tell them also that the place to find their Saboteur is in the cellar, which can be reached by going through the second door in the central room.

If they have the courage to meet their Saboteur, they should go through the door without any preconceptions. The door leads onto a flight of wooden steps that leads downward into the gloom of the cellar. Once they descend these steps, they will find their Saboteur, who may be a living person, a dead person, or even a mythic figure.

Explain to your group that they should not attack the Saboteur, but instead direct a ray of light from their heart onto the Saboteur. When they do so, the Saboteur is transformed into an Ally.

Instruct them that once the transformation has taken place, both they and the former Saboteur should go up together from the cellar. The group members should now come out of their towers into normal waking consciousness, leave the former Saboteur, now Friend and Ally in charge of the tower with special responsibility for keeping the windows shut.

Preliminary Training Technique 3
The final preparatory exercise is based on the concept of vesseling. All of us carry the influences of individuals, religious, political or social groups with us all the time. Sometimes we are conscious of these influences, sometimes not, but so long as we carry the influences, we act as vessels for the individuals or groups who generated them.

An example of vesseling in action might be the child who is encouraged, perhaps even forced, along a particular career path because of his or her parents' expectations. In this case, the child

Another example is the individual who behaves in a certain way because he or she is a member of a particular ethnic grouping—is, for example, black, or Jewish, or White Anglo-Saxon Protestant. Here, the individual is vesseling the particular group.

From these examples, it is evident that we can vessel friends, neighbors, relatives, religions, even whole countries (a process usually referred to as patriotism). In some instances, of course, individuals may be perfectly happy to do so, but in others the vesseling process acts as a barrier to personal freedom or expression. It can also set up conflicts between personal and vesseled expectations which block the sort of inner perceptions we are aiming for in our experiment.

Begin the exercise by discussing the concept of vesseling with your group. It is a difficult concept, so take time to ensure they understand it. Ask each of them to consider who or what he/she may be vesseling, with particular attention to those individuals or groups vesseled unwillingly.

Next, have members of the group select their vessels—a container which is best suited to the things they are vesseling. You can suggest it should be something not too big—a cup or chalice is ideal, although members should be given a free choice. Now, require them to draw the vessel with their "wrong" hand: left hand if they are right-handed, right hand if they are left-handed. Then, have them write in it, still with the wrong hand, what they are vesseling.

When this has been done, guide the group through the following visualization, which should be acted out, standing, with the eyes closed:

You are standing in front of a broad, calm lake of crystal clear healing water. Pull your chosen vessel from your solar plexus—which is where vesseled contents are stored—reach out and empty it with intent into the lake. Empty it completely. Watch the chemical change as the lake water transforms the contents of the vessel into crystal purity.

When your vessel is completely empty and its contents absorbed and transformed by the water, turn your back to the lake and go to the fountain you will see a short distance ahead of you. When you reach the fountain, fill your vessel from it and drink until you feel satisfied. You will find however much you drink, the vessel will always remain full. When you have finished, place your vessel within your heart.

Finally, have each member destroy their drawing of their vessel.

This completes the preliminaries. Your next step is a brief program of sensitivity training, then the time travel experiment itself.

CHAPTER TWENTY-SEVEN

One of the greatest barriers to any unusual experience is the conviction that it is impossible, or—much more usual— that it may be possible for others, but not for the individual concerned. The first three exercises in the sensitivity training program are designed to demonstrate to members of your group that the sort of direct perception we are seeking is indeed possible for them.

Two of the next three exercises involve talents we have already examined—psychometry and dowsing. The third is a simple proof of personal sensitivity. Using the methods described, approximately one group member in three can be taught to psychometrize an object or dowse. Virtually everyone should be able to experience personal sensitivity.

Sensitivity Training Technique 1

For the experience of personal sensitivity, break your group into pairs. Here again, better results accrue if those paired together do not know one another well, or at all. Designate one member of each pair Member A, the other becoming Member B.

Members A and B decide between themselves who will be sender and who receiver. In the following example, Member A is the sender, Member B the receiver.

Member B closes his or her eyes. Member A concentrates on sending angry thoughts towards B for a maximum of two minutes. (If the technique has not worked in that time, it's unlikely to work at all.) Member B raises his or her hand the moment (s)he feels the thoughts. On this signal, Member A ceases to send, whether or not the two minutes have elapsed. Member B should take mental note of how the thoughts were received (sensed as a pain, pressure, itch etc.) and where (in the head, throat, heart, solar plexus, etc.).

Repeat the experiment with the same sender and receiver, but now it is Member A who has closed eyes. Once Member B feels the impact of the thoughts, he or she should strongly visualize a turquoise shield blocking the thoughts. Member A signals with a hand movement when he or she thinks the shield has been raised.

Repeat the sequence a third time, but in place of the visualized shield, have the receiver hold a terminated quartz crystal point upwards at the area where the thought pressure was perceived. (They will quickly discover this acts as an even more effective shield.) Again, Member A should signal the moment he or she perceives the crystal has been raised.

Reverse roles and repeat the entire sequence from the start with Member B now the sender and Member A the receiver.

Now, form a circle and find out what each member of your group loves most. Get them to focus on the object of their affections, then send them back to form the same pairs. Each should take turns to send loving thoughts towards the other. Receivers should take note of how and where the thoughts are received. There is no need to repeat the use of barriers with loving thoughts. When this part of the experiment is complete, break up the pairs and have group members return to their original positions in the room.

Finally, ask if anybody has ever had a negative thought about his or her body. It is rare to find someone who has not. Point out to the group that if they can feel other people's thoughts—and the experiment has just shown them they can—it is small wonder they become ill, sometimes, given that they direct negative thoughts towards themselves. Complete the exercise by getting them to direct loving thoughts to their own body parts, starting with the feet, then working their way up through calves, knees, thighs, genitals, abdomen, and so on. Most groups find this final aspect of the exercise very energizing.

Sensitivity Training Technique 2
Follow this exercise by training in dowsing. Almost anybody can be taught to dowse. Yet, most people find it impossible. This is because almost everyone starts out with the traditional forked stick which is very difficult to use—so difficult that failures are common. Dowsing rods are far easier.

To make a set, all you need are two wire coat-hangers (the sort they use to send back the dry-cleaning) and a pair of wire-cutters.

When you examine the coat-hanger, you will find it is a single piece of stiff wire, twisted into shape. Untwist the wire at the join by the hook and pull apart slightly. Next, bend into a rough L shape. As you do so, you will discover that what you have is a reasonably good L shape in the middle, with messy ends.

Use your wire cutters to trim off the ends and you will be left with one nicely formed L-shaped wire rod. Ideally, the shorter leg of the L should be a little longer than the width of your hand.

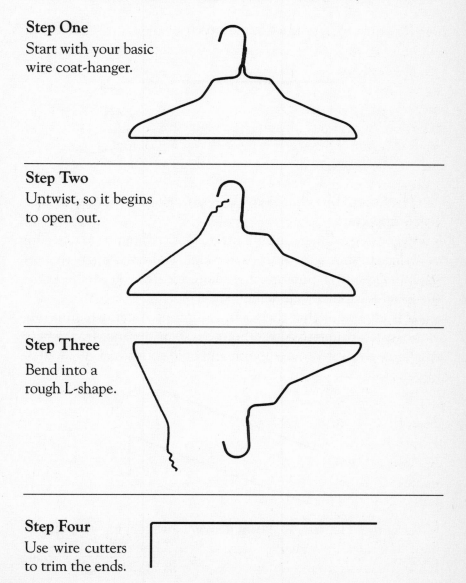

Step One
Start with your basic
wire coat-hanger.

Step Two
Untwist, so it begins
to open out.

Step Three
Bend into a
rough L-shape.

Step Four
Use wire cutters
to trim the ends.

Repeat the same procedure with your second coat hanger, and you will end up with a set of dowsing rods, like this:

To use the rods, hold each one loosely by the short leg, like this:

They should be able to swing easily, left and right, so a light grip is important.

Becoming a dowser takes a little practice, but not much. The best place to start is on any piece of land where you know there is an underground stream or water main. Ideally, you should know the exact location of the watercourse.

It is important that the water is running water, which is one of the easiest things to detect. Start out some distance from where you know the watercourse to run and hold your two rods parallel, like this:

Grip them loosely, as shown above. Now, tucking your elbows in to your sides and moving slowly, walk in a line that will take you across the underground watercourse, roughly at right angles.

As you cross the stream or pipe, you will find that the two long arms of the rods swing slowly inwards and cross, like this:

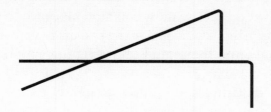

No effort on your part is needed. Hold the rods loosely, walk slowly, and they will swing and cross entirely of their own accord.

Have each member of your group make themselves a set of dowsing rods in this way and organize a brief field trip to test them out. The purpose here is not to undertake scientific experiments in dowsing, only to give your group personal experience of the dowsing effect. If you wish to go a little further than water-course dowsing, you can have them experience metal dowsing using coins.

Start with a coin in plain sight on the floor and have the prospective dowser hold a coin of the same denomination along with the rods. You should get a dowsing reaction as the rods cross over the coin on the floor. Once the reaction is well established by a number of dowsers, have the coin hidden and see how many of the group can find it using only the rods. The technique here is to criss-cross the area where the coin is hidden in a grid pattern until a dowsing reaction arises.

Sensitivity Training Technique 3

The final and most important sensitivity training technique is, of course, psychometry. The technique itself is quite straightforward. Hold an object in both hands resting in your lap, or press it to your forehead. Relax, clear your mind, then simply describe in detail any scenes or impressions that may arise in your imagination. Plastics are difficult to psychometrize, but almost everything else will yield good results. Crystals, including most precious stones, are excellent, as are most metals.

To train your group in psychometry, again split them into pairs. Have one member of the pair attempt to "read" a personal object (such as a watch, a brooch, a ring or other item) belonging to the other. Stress that the most common blockage to psychometry is self-censorship, so encourage the readers to verbalize everything that comes into their minds, however inappropriate it may seem to them.

Stress too that this is a training session, not a scientific experiment, so the person who owns the object should give the reader as much encouragement as possible and in particular confirm any "hits" that may arise. When the reading is complete, have members of the pairs reverse roles.

Make careful note of your star performer in this technique. You will be using him or her as the stimulus for the group's experience in the time travel experiment itself.

CHAPTER TWENTY-EIGHT

Once the sensitivity training is complete, you have only one further preliminary. This is a brief meditation that involves the use of quartz crystals as an imaginative focus. Each member of your group should be equipped with his or her own crystal, which should be in the form of a relatively clear quartz point (as opposed to a cluster). Ideally, individual crystals should be chosen intuitively, but since the New Age movement has made crystals fashionable, there is a chance some of your group members will already own quartz they have chosen in this way. Guide the members of your group through the following meditation:

Sit upright and make sure you are warm, comfortable, and relaxed. Hold your crystal in your hand and allow yourself to be quiet and receptive, breathing regularly and slowly.

With thoughts of love and light, ask your crystal to open an area of its structure so you may enter its form. Imagine your crystal making a special space for you.

Enter your crystal through the doorway of light provided for you, feeling in a state of perfect balance as you explore the interior of your crystal.

Allow all your senses to be open in order to experience your crystal. Touch its sides, its foundation, with your face and hands. Allow your body to lean against a crystal wall. Listen to any sounds you may hear. Feel you are at home and totally welcomed by your crystal. Spend a little while enjoying the attunement.

Now prepare to leave. Thank your crystal for sharing its energies with you.

Focus on your breathing. Wriggle your hands and feet, then return to the present.

Open your eyes.

You are now ready for the experiment itself. As a rough guide, you should allow a period of about two hours to complete it.

The Time Travel Experiment

Before the experiment begins, it is useful to make two temporary appointments. The first is a spokesperson. Although the technique aims to allow each member of the group to sense the same vision, members are often shy at first in expressing their impressions. Thus, the spokesperson functions as the "official" inner eye of the group and acts to prime the pump in the early stages until the remainder of the group gains confidence. In one of the U.K. test groups, two spokespersons were chosen to act in tandem and this proved very effective.

The second appointment is a decision-maker. Should the group find itself unable to agree on a course of action at any particular point in the experiment, members may call on the decision-maker to make an arbitrary choice.

It should be clearly explained that these roles are in no way officials or leaders of the group. The whole point of the technique is mass participation. Each group member must express what they see with their inner eye and take part in discussions and decisions if the experiment is to be successful. The individual who functions as decision-maker must NOT take charge or attempt to lead the group. He or she acts only when group members are at an impasse and cannot decide among themselves what to do. In this instance, the decision-maker will be called on to make a binding decision.

A single individual may function in both appointments. In practice, they are only really important at the beginning of the experience. Once members gain confidence, the group will function increasingly as a single, coherent entity.

Once the appointments have been made, lights should be dimmed and a single candle or night light placed in the center of the room as a focus for the group which sits in a circle around it. The experience begins with the most skilled psychometrist in the group handing the artifact which belongs to the time period you wish to investigate. As he or she does so, the psychometrist describes aloud and in detail any impressions that may arise. You should aid the process by quietly asking questions to clarify the vision. You should, in particular, try to obtain the sort of information that will permit you to build up a detailed scene from the relevant time period associated with the artifact.

When you feel you have enough information, you can allow the psychometrist to relax. You should then ask the group to close their eyes and feed back to them a detailed reprise of the scene described by the psychometrist as if the members of the group were part of it. Here is an example of the sort of description used in one of the test groups and drawn (with embellishments) from an Egyptian artifact:

We stand among the Priests of Sais before House of Amen in the Southern Harim. The great pylons of the Temple tower on either side of us, their host of flag-staves fluttering in a veritable corn-field of brightly colored pennons. Your eyes trace the huge reliefs of Pharaoh, rampant and heroic as a bull, smiting down his ene-mies with an upraised mace.

You look away from the reliefs and back to the flag-staves. They are of wood from Lebanon, like the massive entrance door between the pylons. Thutmose, Father of the God, moves a pace and so they all move, a dignified procession towards the door. Sekhet, on the left of Thutmose, reaches out with that large left hand of his to take the ceremonial staff and knock once on the door. The sound reverberates dully. Then, as he steps back a pace, the door swings open and we are faced by the night-priests.

The Father of the God among the night priests steps forward to present Thutmose with a papyrus scroll, an inventory of Tem-ple contents and effects.

"Is all correct?"

"My Brother, all is correct."

The night priests walk into the sunlight. We pass with the day priests into an open courtyard surrounded by a colonnaded porch. This porch is new, its columns commissioned by the Pharaoh as a gift to the Temple, carved and brightly colored to represent the lo-tus flower. We move from the courtyard down three shallow steps into the hyperstyle, a transverse, columned hall lit only dimly by its clerestory windows. Here the priestesses await us.

The High Priest Khaemuas inclines his head in greeting to the Chief Priestess and she bows briefly back. The priestesses move to take their places among the priests, humming softly to the ac-companiment of the little hand sistras they carried. The group now walks slowly to the sanctuary, the single chamber in which stands the god's own shrine. Like the hyperstyle, the room is dimly lit, but eyes soon adjust so that the heroic frescos on the walls are clearly discerned. The scenes depicted are all of the Pharaoh: the Pharaoh at war, the Pharaoh triumphant, but most of all, the Pharaoh engaged in the great observances of his religion.

The stone shrine of the god is enclosed by two folding wooden doors, fastened with bolts and papyrus strings, sealed with a large clay seal.

A priest steps forward and begins to kindle the censer, a well-formed metal arm, the hand of which holds an incense pot. As the smoke begins to curl upwards, he hands it to the high priest who senses him, the company, the sanctuary, and finally himself. The sweet, heady scent of incense drifts through the chamber.

Khaemuas, the High Priest, sets down the censer and reaches out to break the papyrus string and seal securing the door bolts to the shrine.

"The twin doors of the sky are opened!" he recites. "The two doors of the earth are unclosed. Geb gives greetings, saying to the gods who abide upon their seats: Heaven is opened! The company of gods shines forth! Amen-Ra, Lord of Karnak, is exalted upon his great seat! The Great Nine are exalted upon their seats! Their beauties are thine, O Amen-Ra, Lord of Karnak!"

Within the shrine is an image of the god.

"Purified, purified is Amen-Ra, Lord of Karnak!" Khaemuas proclaims and pours a stream of purest water into the shrine. "Take to thee the water which is in the eye of Horus given to thee is thine eye, given to thee is thy head, given to thee are thy bones, established for thee is thy head upon thy bones in the presence of Geb!" The water streams from the image and is absorbed in the sand....

The idea here is to dramatize the findings of the psychometrist, presenting them in the form of a vivid picture in which the group members are already present. It is important to maintain agreement with the psychometrist's vision and/or historical accuracy, but unless the picture you present is colorful and vivid, members of your group may have difficulty in visualizing it.

Once you feel you have clearly established the scene, have your group members open their eyes, then ask quietly where they want to go. In the example above, they may decide to explore the remainder of the temple complex or leave it altogether and explore the city of which it was a part. Where they go should be left entirely to the group's own judgment.

Once they leave the environment you have initially established, you should cease to describe their environment, but instead ask the spokesperson what the group is seeing and encourage other individual group members to describe what visions are arising before their own inner eyes. With a little patient questioning and encouragement, you will find that the group settles into what is largely a single vision. Allow them to wander at will through this vision, taking note of details as they go along.

Coincidentally, all test groups using this program spontaneously concluded their experiments after an approximate two-hour period—members felt the time had come to return to the present. If this does not happen in your group, you should select a suitable stage to intervene and suggest quietly that they return to the room and re-establish themselves in the present. It is a good idea for members to eat something immediately afterwards—even a cup of tea and a biscuit—as there is a distinct tendency towards vagueness and dreaminess following an experiment of this type.

If the experience of the test groups is typical, members will find the experiment enjoyable and often exciting, but the really interesting part comes afterwards. This is when you analyze your records of the trip against historical evidence and discover whether or not you have engaged in a pleasant fantasy ... or managed literally to travel in time.

APPENDIX A
Archaeological Dating

When archaeologists make a find of any sort, their first and most obvious problem is to date it. The problem is compounded when it comes to dating prehistoric finds, that is, artifacts laid down before the invention of writing.

An early breakthrough in dating methods came with the development of the Three Age System, which recognized that in deep prehistory, stone tools were replaced by bronze, then iron. This meant that a strata of stone finds could be confidently dated to an earlier era than a similar strata containing bronze. As we have already seen, bronze and iron are not notable survivors, so the Three Age System is of limited use, but for a long time it was all the archaeologists had, and they refined it through careful analysis of technology and style. Based on the assumption that tools and weapons evolve from crude beginnings to a more sophisticated form, it became possible to develop a chronological sequence. Such sequences were codified and, with the addition of pottery and art works, a useful timetable of history evolved.

However, style analysis was a long way from producing pinpoint accuracy and in many instances was of no use at all. The search for more accurate dating methods continued, and in the twentieth century came a series of scientific discoveries. Among the earliest of these was something called dendrochronology, an impressive term which hides an observation known to every boy scout: you can tell the age of a felled tree by counting the rings in its trunk.

In archaeology, what the experts look for is an overlap of patterns seen in living trees with ring patterns in old wood. From this simple idea has emerged a system of dating valid for 7,000 years (i.e., up to about 5000 B.C.) Unfortunately, it is only useful for the dating of wooden objects.

Early twentieth-century scientists added a second approach which greatly extended their chronological investigations—varve dating. A varve is the annual layer of sediment laid down on lake beds at the edge of glaciers. Counting varves, like tree rings, permitted the accurate dating of certain events, such as the ending of the last Ice Age.

Like dendrochronology, varve dating has obvious limitations, and the scientists continued to search for ways in which more artifacts could be more accurately dated. The breakthrough came almost midway through the century when, in the late 1940s, byproducts of nuclear research presented archaeologists with three of the most useful tools they could have imagined—thermoluminescence, potassium-argon. and radiocarbon dating.

One of the most common finds at archaeological sites is pottery. Pottery is made from clay which, like many other materials, exhibits a low, but measurable, level of background radioactivity. This radioactivity has the effect, over time, of releasing electrons, but the electrons remain trapped in the clay until it is heated, which is exactly what happens when a clay pot is fired. When heating takes place, the electrons are released as light. This process is known as thermoluminescence, light released by heat.

If you take fired clay and heat it again, measuring the light released allows you to calculate how much time has elapsed since the first firing. This is the essence of thermoluminescence dating.

Radiocarbon dating is a far more familiar term. It is based on the discovery that carbon exhibits a steady rate of radioactive decay. Measure the amount of the decay, and you measure the life of the carbon. Since carbon is found in most organic materials—bone, shell, and other plant and animal remains—it is obviously useful to date sites where such remains are found. Although as popular with the media as it is with archaeologists, radiocarbon dating has two important limitations. First, it can only be used to date organic remains. It cannot, for example, directly date a menhir at Brittany. Secondly, it can only be applied successfully to remains less than 40,000 years old.

Potassium-argon dating works in essentially the same way as radiocarbon dating (i.e. it measures a known rate of radioactive decay), but in this case the method is limited to volcanic materials. While this places obvious limitations on its use, the temporal reach of the method is millions of years.

APPENDIX B
Historical Anachronisms

The illustrations below offer evidence (or at least food for thought) for the proposition that we humans have somehow walked the Earth long before evolution gives us any right to.

Figure A. A striated metal sphere found in Precambrian mineral deposits in the Western Transvaal region of South Africa.

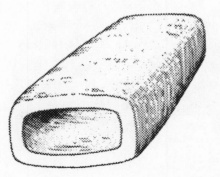

Figure B. A metallic tube found in a 65-million-year-old French chalk bed.

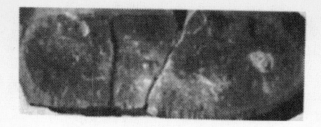

Figure C. A shoelike print found in Cambrian shale by W. Meister in Antelope Spring, Utah; 1968.

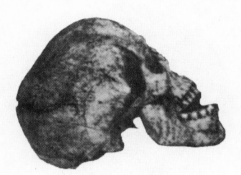

Figure D. A modern human skull found in a possibly late Early Pleistocene soil layer by H. Reck at Olduvai Gorge; 1913.

Figure E. Excavated human skull found in an Early Pleistocene formation in Buenos Aires; 1896.

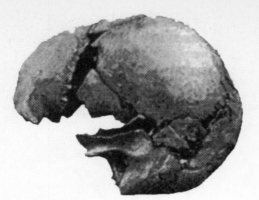

Figure F. A modern human skull found in a Middle Pliocene stratum by G. Ragazzoni in Castenedolo, Italy; 1880.

Figure G. Artist's rendition of a coin found in a 200,000-400,000-year-old soil layer. Illinois; 1871.

Figure H. A shoe-like print, complete with stitching, in Triassic era rock. Reported by W. H. Ballou in Nevada; 1922.

Idaho State Historical Society

Figure I. A clay figure excavated from Plio-Pleistocene strata at Nampa, Idaho, during a well drilling; 1889.

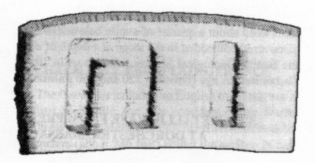

Figure J. Embossed figures found in marble quarried from a depth of sixty to seventy feet, from a site near Philadelphia; 1830.

GLOSSARY

ANTI-MATTER: A type of matter consisting of anti-particles which annihilates normal matter (and itself) on contact.

ANTI-PARTICLE: Subatomic particle having an equal and opposite charge to its paired particle.

AUSTRALOPITHECINE: Extinct South African ape with human-like characteristics, generally accepted as an evolutionary precursor of humanity.

BIG BANG: Name for what is currently the most popular theory among physicists on the origin of the universe.

BLACK HOLE: The remnant of a collapsed star of such magnitude that its gravity allows nothing to escape, not even light.

BROWNIAN MOTION: The movement of dust particles caused by their collision with water molecules.

BUBBLE-CHAMBER: A device which shows the tracks left by the movement of subatomic particles.

CAMBRIAN: Geological period of the Earth's history.

CARBONIFEROUS: Geological period of the Earth's history.

CHERENKOV RADIATION: Radiation emitted by any faster-than-light charged particle.

CLOSED TIMELIKE LINE: A geometric construct, predicted mathematically, which winds through space-time to return to its point of origin in time as well as space.

COMPUTER MODEL: Computer program which seeks to emulate a particular aspect of reality.

DEADLY ZONE: An area surrounding a Tipler Cylinder in which the fabric of space-time is so distorted that nothing could survive.

DENDROCHRONOLOGY: A method of dating by counting tree rings.

DEVONIAN: Geological period of the Earth's history.

DNA: Basic building block of organic life.

DOUBLE SLIT EXPERIMENT: An experiment in quantum physics which some physicists believe indicates the existence of parallel universes.

EINSTEIN-ROSEN BRIDGE: A mathematical construction linking a Black Hole with a hypothetical White Hole in a parallel universe.

ELECTRON: A subatomic particle.

EPR EFFECT: The observation that there is a fundamental connection between twin particles even when they are separated.

ESP: Extra Sensory Perception, a term used in scientific research to denote various psychical talents.

GREEN BANK FORMULA: Formula which attempts to calculate the number of advanced civilizations in our galaxy.

HEISENBERG'S UNCERTAINTY PRINCIPLE: An encapsulation of the fact that you can measure the speed or the location of a subatomic particle, but not both.

HOMINID: Early proto-human.

HOMO ERECTUS: An early form of humanity.

HOMO HABILIS: An early form of humanity.

HOMO SAPIENS SAPIENS: Modern humanity.

IMAGINARY SPACE: The way physicists (sometimes) experience time.

JURASSIC: Geological period of the Earth's history.

KAON: A subatomic particle.

MESOZOIC: Geological period of the Earth's history.

MINOWSKI EQUATIONS: Mathematical formulae based on Einstein's relativity theory.

MORLEY-MICHELSON EXPERIMENT: Experiment which showed the speed of light to be constant.

MUON: A subatomic particle.

NEANDERTHAL: Early form of humanity now extinct.

NEUTRINO: A subatomic particle.

NEUTRON: A subatomic particle.

NEUTRON STAR: A collapsed star composed of hyper-dense, extremely heavy matter.

NON-EUCLIDEAN GEOMETRY: Any geometry which is not based on the 'self-evident' axioms of the Greek Euclid.

NUCLEUS: The heart of the atom.

PALEOZOIC: Geological period of the Earth's history.

PARALLEL UNIVERSES: Space-time continua now believed by many physicists to lie outside our own.

PENNSYLVANIAN: Geological period of the Earth's history.

PHOTON: Subatomic particle of light.

PION: A subatomic particle.

PLANCK'S CONSTANT: A fundamental value related to energy quanta.

PLIOCENE ERA: Geological period of the Earth's history.

POINCARÉ'S RETURN: A theorem which indicates that a closed system will always return to its original state given enough time.

POSITRON: A subatomic particle.

PRECAMBRIAN: Geological period of the Earth's history.

PROBABILITY WAVES: A postulate of quantum physics which suggests subatomic particles are actually wave forms describing the various possibilities of manifestation.

PROTON: A subatomic particle.

PSYCHOMETRY: A process by which the history of an object may be intuitively sensed by handling it.

QUANTUM TUNNELING: A theoretical process by means of which it might be possible to pass from one parallel universe to another.

RELATIVITY: Umbrella term relating to Einstein's insights into the nature of the universe.

SCHRÖDINGER'S CAT: An unfortunate but imaginary animal used to test certain postulates of quantum physics.

SCHWARZSCHILD RADIUS: The point at which a collapsing star becomes a Black Hole.

SETI: Search for Extra Terrestrial Intelligence.

SINGULARITY: Any point in the solution to a mathematical formula where values reach infinity. Often refers to calculations about the nature of Black Holes—hence its use to describe an area of the Black Hole itself.

SOCIETY FOR PSYCHICAL RESEARCH: An organization set up in Victorian Britain (and later America) to promote the scientific investigation of psychical phenomena. Both the British and American Societies are still highly active.

SPACE-TIME: Space and time considered as a single continuum.

SUBATOMIC PARTICLE: Inner constituent of the atom.

TACHYON: A postulated subatomic particle that travels freely through time.

TIPLER CYLINDER: Hypothetical time machine designed by physicist Frank Tipler.

TRIASSIC: Geological period of the Earth's history.

VIKING: Unmanned spacecraft.

VOYAGER: Unmanned spacecraft.

WAVE-PARTICLE DUALITY: Term coined to describe the fact that particles sometimes behave like particles and sometimes like waves.

WHITE DWARF: A collapsed star.

WORMHOLE: Hypothetical "tunnel" through space or time.

ZENER PACK: Special pack of twenty-five cards used in psychical and ESP research.

ZERO TIME PARTICLE: A subatomic particle for which time has no existence; e.g. a photon.

BIBLIOGRAPHY

Adamski, George and Desmond Leslie. *Flying Saucers Have Landed*. London: Neville Spearman, 1970.

Beiser, Arthur. *The Earth*. New York: Time Life, 1964.

Bohm, David. *Wholeness and the Implicate Order*. London: Ark Books, 1983.

Bradbury, Ray. "The Sound of Thunder." Playboy Magazine. June, 1956

Brennan, J. H. *Nostradamus, Visions of the Future*. London: Aquarian Press, 1993.

————. *The Atlantis Technique*. Ireland: Maggot Press, 1994.

Briggs, John and F. David Peat. *Turbulent Mirror*. New York: Harper & Row, 1990.

Capra, Fritjof. *Uncommon Wisdom*. London: Fontana, 1989.

Chapman, Robert. *Unidentified Flying Objects*. London: Arthur Barker, 1969.

Chetham, Erika. *The Prophecies of Nostradamus*. London: Corgi Books, 1989.

Chown, Marcus. *Afterglow of Creation*. London: Arrow Books, 1993.

Cianchi, Marco. *Leonardo's Machines*. Florence, Italy: Becocci Editore, 1986.

Coveney, Peter and Roger Highfield. *The Arrow of Time*. London: Flamingo Books, 1991.

Cremo, Michael A. and Richard L. Thompson. *Forbidden Archaeology*. San Diego: Bhaktivedanta Institude, 1993.

Davies, Paul. *God and the New Physics*. London: Penguin Books, 1987.

Dunne, J. W. *An Experiment with Time*. London: Faber and Faber, 1958.

Epstein, Gerald. *Studies in Non-Deterministic Psychology*. New York: Human Sciences Press, 1980.

Fogarty, Quentin. *Let's Hope They're Friendly*. Australia: Angus & Robertson, 1982.

Gamow, George. *A Planet Called Earth*. London: Macmillan, 1964.

Gleick, James. *Chaos*. London: Cardinal, 1988.

Goodman, Jeffrey. *Psychic Archaeology*. London: Panther Books, 1979.

Greenhouse, Herbert B. *Premonitions: a Leap into the Future*. London: Turnstone Books, 1972.

Heard, Gerald. *The Riddle of the Flying Saucers*. London: Carroll and Nicholson, 1950.

Hoffman, Michael A. *Egypt before the Pharaohs*. London: Ark Books, 1984.

Hogue, John. *Nostradamus and the Millennium*. London: Bloomsbury, 1987.

Hotton, Nicholas III.*The Evidence of Evolution*. London: Penguin Books, 1973.

Hynek, J. Allen. *The UFO Experience*. London: Corgi Books, 1974.

Kaku, Michio. *Hyperspace*. New York: Oxford University Press, 1994.

Keyhoe, Donald E. *Flying Saucers from Outer Space*. London: Tandem Books, 1970.

Morris, Richard.*The Nature of Reality*. New York: Noonday Press, 1988.

Mysteries of the Unexplained. Edited by Carroll C. Calkins. London: Reader's Digest Books, 1982.

Regis, Ed. *Great Mambo Chicken and the Transhuman Condition*. London: Penguin Books, 1992.

Ridley, B. K. *Time, Space and Things*. London: Penguin Books, 1976.

Roe, Derek. *Prehistory Roe*. London: Paladin, 1971.

Sacks, Oliver. *The Man Who Mistook His Wife for a Hat*. London: Pan Books, 1986.

Sanderson, Ivan. *Things and More Things*. New York: Pyramid Books, 1967.

Simpson, G. G. *The Meaning of Evolution*. New York: Bantam Books, 1971.

Spencer, John. *Perspectives*. London: Futura Books, 1990.

Talbot, Michael. *The Holographic Universe*. New York: HarperCollins, 1992.

Taylor, John. *Black Holes: the End of the Universe?* London: Souvenir Press, 1973.

Thomas, Paul. *Flying Saucers through the Ages*. London: Tandem, 1973.

Toynbee, Arnold. *A Study of History*. London: Oxford University Press, 1954.

Weldon, John and Zola Levitt. *UFOs: What on Earth is Happening?* New York: Bantam Books, 1976.

Welfare, Simon and John Fairley. *Arthur C. Clarke's Mysterious World*. London: Fontana Books, 1982.

Wilford, John Noble. *The Riddle of the Dinosaur*. London: Faber and Faber, 1986.

Wilson, Colin. *Beyond the Occult*. London: Bantam Press, 1988.

————. *Mysteries*. London: Panther Books, 1979.

————. *The Occult*. London: Grafton Books, 1989.

————. *The Supernatural*. London: Robinson Publishing, 1991.

Wolf, Fred Alan. *Parallel Universes*. New York: Touchstone Books, 1990.

Zukav, Gary. *The Dancing Wu Li Masters*. London: Fontana Books, 1982.

INDEX

Stay in Touch. . .

Llewellyn publishes hundreds of books on your favorite subjects

On the following pages you will find listed some books now available on related subjects. Your local bookstore stocks most of these and will stock new Llewellyn titles as they become available. We appreciate your patronage!

Order by Phone

Call toll-free within the U.S. and Canada, 1–800–THE MOON.
In Minnesota call (612) 291–1970.
We accept Visa, MasterCard, and American Express.

Order by Mail

Send the full price of your order (MN residents add 7% sales tax) in U.S. funds to:
Llewellyn Worldwide
P.O. Box 64383, Dept. L007–9
St. Paul, MN 55164–0383, U.S.A.

Postage and Handling

- $4.00 for orders $15.00 and under
- $5.00 for orders over $15.00
- No charge for orders over $100.00

We ship via UPS in the continental United States. We cannot ship to P.O. boxes. Orders shipped to Alaska, Hawaii, Canada, Mexico, and Puerto Rico will be sent by first-class mail.
International orders: Airmail—add freight equal to price of each book to the total price of order, plus $5.00 for each non-book item (audiotapes, etc.). Surface mail—Add $1.00 per item.
Allow 4–6 weeks for all deliveries. Postage and handling rates subject to change.

Group Discounts

We offer a 20% quantity discount to group leaders or agents. You must order a minimum of five copies of the same book to get our special quantity price.

Free Catalog

Get a free copy of our color catalog, *New Worlds of Mind and Spirit*. Subscribe for just $10.00 in the United States and Canada ($20.00 overseas, first class mail). Many bookstores carry New Worlds—ask for it!

Prices subject to change without notice.

STRANGE ENCOUNTERS
UFOs, Aliens & Monsters Among Us
Curt Sutherly

UFOs and ghost lights … sky quakes and strange disappearances … phantom creatures and cryptozoological oddities … all of these mysterious phenomena make us acutely aware of how little we really understand our world and the universe beyond. *Strange Encounters* was written by an experienced journalist and ufologist who has interviewed and personally investigated many of the remarkable, yet true, events he documents in this collection.

Take a weird journey into the unexplained with 15 gripping stories gathered from the author's own journalistic investigations. From alien encounters to eyewitness disappearances to the Mars probe failure, these are puzzles without real solutions. But Curt Sutherly points out significant parallels between sightings in different parts of the United States, which add up to a pattern of strange occurrences—based on reliable sources—that cannot be intelligently dismissed. If you want the truth about these mysterious sightings and who's attempting to cover them up, then this book will wholly engross you.

ISBN: 1-56718-699-8, 272 pp., mass market $5.99

PSYCHIC EMPOWERMENT
A 7-Day Plan for Self-Development
Joe Slate, Ph.D.

Use 100% of your mind power in just one week! You've heard it before: each of us is filled with an abundance of untapped power—yet we only use *one-tenth* of its potential. Now a clinical psychologist and famed researcher in parapsychology shows you *how* to probe your mind's psychic faculties and manifest your capacity to *access* the higher planes of the mind.

The psychic experience validates your true nature and connects you to your inner knowing. Dr. Slate reveals the life-changing nature of psychic phenomena—including telepathy, out-of-body experiences and automatic writing. At the same time, he shows you how to develop a host of psychic abilities including psychokinesis, crystal gazing, and table tilting.

The last section of the book outlines his accelerated 7-Day Psychic Development Plan through which you can unleash your innate power and wisdom without delay.

1-56718-635-1, 6 x 9, 256 pp., softbound $12.95

Prices subject to change without notice.